CHICAGO PUBLIC LIBRARY
BUSINESS / SCIENCE / TECHNOLOGY
400 S. STATE ST.   60605 SJF

The
Racing
Game

D1570062

The
Racing
Game

Marvin B. Scott

With a new introduction by Jaime Suchlicki

ALDINETRANSACTION
A Division of Transaction Publishers
New Brunswick (U.S.A.) and London (U.K.)

New material this edition copyright © 2005 by Transaction Publishers, New Brunswick, New Jersey. Copyright © 1968 by Marvin B. Scott.

All rights reserved under International and Pan-American Copyright Conventions. No part of this book may be reproduced or transmitted in any form or by any means, electronic or mechanical, including photocopy, recording, or any information storage and retrieval system, without prior permission in writing from the publisher. All inquiries should be addressed to AldineTransaction, A Division of Transaction Publishers, Rutgers—The State University, 35 Berrue Circle, Piscataway, New Jersey 08854-8042. www.transactionpub.com

This book is printed on acid-free paper that meets the American National Standard for Permanence of Paper for Printed Library Materials.

Library of Congress Catalog Number: 2005048529
ISBN: 0-202-30809-X
Printed in the United States of America

Library of Congress Cataloging-in-Publication Data

Scott, Marvin B.
    The racing game / Marvin B. Scott ; with a new introduction by Jaime
    Suchlicki.
        p. cm.
    Originally published: Chicago : Aldine Pub. Co., 1968. With new introd.
    ISBN 0-202-30809-X (pbk. : alk. paper)
    1. Horse racing. 2. Horse racing—Betting. I. Title.

SF334.S35 2005
798.4—dc22

                                                    2005048529

BST,
OPN

R0407360015

CHICAGO PUBLIC LIBRARY
BUSINESS / SCIENCE / TECHNOLOGY
400 S. STATE ST.   60605   58F

For My Dad,
Who Introduced Me to
the Social World of Horse Racing

CONTENTS

ALDINETRANSACTION INTRODUCTION

And they're off! The thoroughbreds thunder down the track; the riders jockey for position; the owners breathe anxiously; the public cheers, hoping for a wining ticket.

In a little over a minute much disappointment and some happy faces. This race is over. The next one will start soon. Hope is eternal.

The "sport of kings" has captivated the imagination of rich and poor alike for centuries. Sea Biscuit showed us all what dreams are made of. A small, wretched, rejected horse became a champion. The faith of an owner and the hard work and expertise of a trainer transformed a loser with "heart" into a champion for all times. The recent film allowed millions to relive the sad experiences of the Depression, the agony of hopelessness and defeat, and the glory of Sea Biscuit's victories.

This new edition of Marvin Scott's classic, *The Racing Game*, takes us inside the action. Some two decades of personal, close contact with almost every aspect of horseracing, combined with three years of systematic observation and statistical tabulations, provides the basic data.

The result is an eminently readable, detailed study, a point of departure for anyone interested in horseracing and the people connected with racing.

But this book is more than a casual book on horseracing. It is a sociological analysis of the people involved in this business—the jockeys, trainers, owners, track personnel, and the betting public. Scott uses "game theory" to highlight the tension involved in the successes and failures associated with each group.

The Racing Game is above all a study in social organization. Scott's analysis differs from other investigations into horseracing. Other works focus on the history of the sport, its folklore, or the techniques of picking a winner. This book constitutes a study in the organization of information that leads to Scott's major theoretical assumption: the study of social organization is the study of the organization of information.

Information, or disinformation, is at the core of horseracing. Wining is not necessarily the goal of all the performers, all the time. There are times to win and times to lose. Losing increases the betting odds of a horse on a future race and, therefore, brings a better payoff. Either jockeys or trainers, or both, engage in deception. They both control appearances and outcomes. The game is, therefore, usually played in "terms of strategies of concealment."

This happens perhaps more often in cheaper, claiming races where the purses are smaller. In better, more expensive races where the purses are larger jockeys and trainers are less likely to manipulate their horses. In these races winning becomes the real objective and deception plays a lesser role.

Scott's chapter on the audience shows that the betting public "perceives the race as a natural event, capable of being determined by analysis." The public believes that the various sources of printed information and the data available allow them to make calculated selections that could lead to successful gambling. Scott shows that the manipulation of information makes this more difficult, or at least more challenging.

The Racing Game is a book to be read with interest by the social scientist and with concern by the betting public. Yet this second edition of this fascinating book is an important addition to the literature, a must for anyone interest in horseracing.

Jaime Suchlicki
Emilio Bacardi Moreau Distinguished Professor of History
University of Miami
February 2005

PREFACE

Heads apart, three glistening thoroughbreds thunder toward the finish line, their riders crouched low with whip arms flailing. As the action on the track reaches its conclusion, the shouting of the fans rises to an ear-splitting crescendo. Driving toward the wire, the three horses are bunched so closely that it is a tossup which will win. To the fans, this is a magnificent struggle of nature—flesh and blood and pounding hoofs—clearly, nature in the raw.

But what appears a natural reality also can be viewed as the construction of man's activities. That is, natural events are often as they ought to be because they are the products of human constructions: social organization makes nature follow our needs.

To see a close race as a system-generated reality (that is, as the product of human activities), we need only to mention the routine activities of three participants found at every race track: the trainer, the racing secretary, and the placing judge.

In the pursuit of his own self-interest, a trainer of a horse may unwittingly contribute to making the race more enjoyable for the viewers. A trainer, wishing to disguise the true ability of his animal, may instruct the jockey to win by the narrowest possible margin. The unintended consequence of this is to give those at trackside what they want: "a real horse race"—a sports cliche defined as an event where the contenders are bunched close together at the finish.

The racing secretary is a track employee who writes the eligibility rules for horses entering a race. His function is to bring together equally matched horses to ensure close races, and his success is measured in terms of the frequency of close finishes. And in fact, most races are seen as closely matched affairs.

The placing judge also contributes to the illusion of the natural reality of closeness by designating as a "photo finish" any distance less than half a length that may separate the first, second, or third horse passing the finish wire. The placing judge generally calls anything resembling a close event a "photo finish." When that decision is made, the word "photo" flashes on the infield board and the track announcer will report: "The result of the race is a photo. Please hold all pari-mutuel tickets until the officials have examined the photograph."

Thus, the trainer, the track secretary, and the placing judge engage in activities that have the consequence of producing a photo finish, enhancing the enjoyment and involvement of the spectators. In this manner, social organization has made natural reality conform to our needs. Nature, as it were, imitates art.

As our brief account of the presumed natural realities of a close race indicates, this is a study in social organization. This analysis differs from previous investigations of horse racing, both popular and scientific. Students of horse racing have either focused on its history,[1] its anecdotal folklore,[2] or the "scientific techniques" of picking winners.[3] Several sociological analyses have been concerned with the nature and functions of horse race gambling.[4] My study seeks to complement those other works by focusing on horse racing as a type of social organization.

1. William H. P. Robertson, *The History of Thoroughbred Racing in America* (Englewood Cliffs, N.J.: Prentice-Hall, 1964).

2. Joe H. Palmer, *This Was Racing* (New York: Barnes and Noble, 1953).

3. The two best "how to" books on beating the races are, interestingly, written by Ph.D.'s. See Ira S. Cohen and George D. Stephens, *Scientific Handicapping* (Englewood Cliffs, N.J.: Prentice-Hall, 1963), and Burton P. Fabricand, *Horse Sense* (New York: David McKay, 1965).

4. See Edward C. Devereux, Jr., "Gambling and the Social Structure—A Sociological Study of Lotteries and Horse Racing in Contemporary America" (unpublished doctoral dissertation, Harvard University, 1949);

I wish to express here my indebtedness to the many people who helped make the book possible. This book owes its profoundest debt to my two great teachers, Herbert Blumer and Erving Goffman; to my peers who, during our days as graduate students at Berkeley, made life a glorious adventure of the mind; and especially to my fellow members of a yearlong, informal ethno-methodology seminar: Sherri Cavan, Henry Elliot, Harvey Sacks, Emanuel Schegloff, David Sudnow, Roy Turner, and Carl Werthman. With respect to this work, I am especially indebted to Roy Turner, who not only encouraged me in this project, but whose detailed commentary vastly improved the manuscript.

The manuscript benefited greatly from the always insightful commentary of Howard Becker, Herbert Blumer, Sherri Cavan, David Matza, and Irving Piliavin.

Finally, there is Erving Goffman, who guided me in every stage of this project. Throughout the manuscript, I have adopted aspects of his theoretical ideas, though often for different analytical purposes. I should like to acknowledge my dependence upon his work without implicating him in any way with the uses I have made of it. But if the reader finds in the following pages something of theoretical value, credit should go to him even where I have failed to acknowledge this credit.

M. B. S.

John Richard O'Hare, *The Socio-Economic Aspects of Horse Racing* (Washington, D.C.: Catholic University Press, 1945); and the short useful study by Robert D. Herman, "Gambling as Work: A Sociological Study of the Race Track," in his edited work, *Gambling* (New York: Harper and Row, 1967).

1.

INTRODUCTION

The social world of horse racing evolves around problems of *information*.[1]

Information may be defined simply as what a social actor knows about a situation. At the outset we may distinguish two kinds of information: the first involves an actor's knowledge about the overall situation; the second is what he knows in common with other actors with whom he is in interaction.

These two kinds of information imply two kinds of ignorance.[2] What actors do not know about the workings of the total situation may be called *organizational ignorance*. The degree of organizational ignorance will vary for different actors depending on their positions in an organization. What actors do not know in common with other actors with whom they interact may be called *interactional ignorance*. For any two interactants—say, ego and alter—what ego is ignorant of is what he doesn't know that alter

1. The concept of information is usefully discussed in Jurgen Ruesch and Gregory Bateson, *Communication, The Social Matrix of Psychiatry* (New York: W. W. Norton, 1951), especially chapters 6 and 11. This book also contains a rich, though dated, bibliography on the subject.

2. For a theoretical statement on the concept of ignorance see Wilbert E. Moore and Melvin M. Tumin, "Some Social Functions of Ignorance," *American Sociological Review*, 14 (December 1949), pp 787–795, and Louis Schneider, "The Role of the Category of Ignorance in Sociological Theory," *American Sociological Review*, 27 (August 1962), pp. 492–508.

knows, and vice versa. In the social world of horse racing, both kinds of ignorance are widely prevalent.

Besides the prevalence of organizational and interactional ignorance, much information that is available in horse racing possesses the property of *ambiguity*.[3] To illustrate, consider a bit of information that race track gamblers believe to be very important in betting decisions: a horse has been entered in a race in which he will be running against animals that are markedly inferior to those with which he is generally matched. Now here is the rub and the nub of the matter: this bit of information is subject to two opposing interpretations. On one hand, a bettor may interpret this information to mean that a horse will win easily, because "everyone knows" that higher grade animals beat those of a lower grade. On the other hand, he may interpret this information to mean that the horse stands little chance of winning, because "everyone knows" that horsemen enter their animals in cheaper-than-usual races only when their chargers have become unsound.

Given the imperfectness and incompleteness of information—as implied by the prevalence of organizational and interactional ignorance—and given the ambiguity of available information—as illustrated above—how do horse racing participants go about their business? How can they make decisions with such poor information? How, indeed, is continuous action made possible? Clearly, we are confronted with another version of the Hobbesian question of how social order is possible.[4]

The curious fact about horse racing is that the participants do not act as if they were incompletely informed—not at all. Everything that is needed to pursue a consistent line of action is somehow known. How this is possible constitutes a major mystery that I wish to explore.

3. For a systematic discussion and application of the concept of ambiguity see Neil J. Smelser, *Theory of Collective Behavior* (New York: Free Press of Glencoe, 1963), pp. 63ff and *passim*.

4. The best contemporary statement is to be found in Talcott Parsons, *The Structure of Social Action* (Glencoe, Ill.: The Free Press, 1949), chapter 3.

More specifically, the questions I wish to explore are: What interpretive devices are employed by the participants to obtain information? What tactics are routinely used by which they encode and decode pertinent messages? How do they determine the probable value of information? What are the patterns of information exchange? What resources .are available by which innovations develop to produce information?

Answers to these questions constitute a study in the *organization of information.* All this leads to my major theoretical assumption: *the proper study of social organization is the study of the organization of information.*

Having stated the type of data with which I will be concerned primarily, the next issue involves the theoretical model suitable for investigating the social organization of horse racing. Briefly, I have chosen to investigate the social organization of horse racing in terms of a game model in its simple social-psychological form.[5]

Beginning with the notion of the game as our model of an interaction system, we can think of race track happenings as game-generated events and the players as game-generated identities. Like all games, the racing game consists of rules that provide a framework of possible actions. Within the framework of these rules, the players can make certain moves. The players will employ different strategies depending upon their interest in the game (that is, the outcomes and rewards they are pursuing).

In this context, the players will face certain recurrent problems. To cope with these problems, standard orientations emerge. Persons who align their activities in terms of one of these standard orientations are identified and typed by other players. While

5. Most important for the purposes of this study is the theoretical position of Thomas C. Schelling, *The Strategy of Conflict* (New York: Oxford University Press, 1963). Some of Schelling's ideas have been greatly expanded and refined in Erving Goffman's unpublished manuscript, "Strategic Interaction and Communication." Throughout this study I have leaned heavily on Goffman's paper. Another important statement of games in their simple social-psychological form is to be found in John W. Thibaut and Harold H. Kelley, *The Social-Psychology of Groups* (New York: John Wiley, 1959).

the social actors tend to reify these types, the scientific observer must keep in mind that these types are simply conventional responses or orientations to a set of recurrent conditions.

What is generated in the world of horse racing is an *information game*. The information game is a game of *strategy*. That is, each player in deciding on a course of action takes into account that other players are engaged in the same sort of accounting. The players in this game are concerned with *strategic information*, which is not shared by the players in interaction; if this information were shared, the nature of the interaction would be radically different.[6] Since information is a crucial feature of this game, much activity will be devoted toward discovering, concealing, and using information. Taken together, these *patterns* of interaction make up the information game, and the *mode* of interaction characteristic of the information game will be called *strategic interaction*.[7]

For the vast majority of players, the object of this game is to obtain "reliable information," which will enable them to make winning bets. Each bet may be called a play, and the game-generated event where the play occurs is the race. To make a successful play is to "beat the race." A continual pattern of beating the race gives rise to the much sought state of "beating the game" or "beating the system."

The player's effort to beat the race is constrained by a peculiar feature of horse racing: namely, the information game is played under a system of *self-destroying information*. That is, the very activity of using reliable information destroys its value. Even if the player knows for certain that only one horse in a race will be sent "all out" to win, he will be constrained from fully capitalizing on this information. The payoff for any horse depends on the amount of money bet on it. Thus the more money bet, the lower the odds and the smaller the payoff. Because no player can beat the game by beating one race, the player must continually renew his efforts at assessments for each play. As a

6. This notion of "strategic information" is used in accord with Goffman's conceptualization, *ibid.*

7. This concept, too, is borrowed from Goffman, *ibid.*

result, patterns of strategic interaction remain persistent features of the game.

My task in the following chapters is to clarify and illustrate these rather abstract remarks. In the conclusion, I will review in detail what I have said about horse racing in terms of an information game.

Before concluding this introduction, I think a personal and methodological note is in order.

For my own part, I have found in horse racing a never-ending source of wonderment. Largely because of familial connections, I have had more than fifteen years of informational access to almost every aspect of horse racing. During this period I have "rail-birded" with clockers as they timed the 6 A.M. workouts of horses. I have licked stamps for a touting agency. I have spent summers traveling on the road with jockeys, trainers, and grooms. I have sat countless hours in horse rooms, legal and illegal, observing the scene. During afternoons at the track, I have spent about equal time in the three main areas of observation—the grandstand, the clubhouse, and the turf club. True, for the greater part of this time I viewed the arena of horse racing with a sociological naivete. But these early experiences furnished a vocabulary that enabled me to participate easily in the social world of horse racing during three years of systematic and sociologically informed observations.

Once I began systematic observations, a knotty problem arose: What to record and when to stop? In my observations, I was sensitive to anything that bore on the conceptual categories developed by Goffman,[8] plus any hypotheses that were developed in the field. When the field notes piled up, I was forced to come to terms with the problem of criterion of an adequate description: When, I asked, does the field worker know that he has enough data?

8. In particular I was guided by the concepts found in the following works by Goffman: *Presentation of Self in Everyday Life* (Anchor Paperback, 1959); *Encounters* (Indianapolis: Bobbs-Merrill, 1961); *Behavior in Public Places* (New York: Free Press of Glencoe, 1963).

One solution to this problem is implied in Ward H. Good-enough's conception of culture. According to Goodenough, a society's culture consists "of whatever it is one has to know or believe in order to operate in a manner acceptable to its members and do so in any role that they accept for any one of themselves." [9] Thus, an adequate description should be sufficiently detailed so that one could write a set of instructions enabling a stranger to reproduce the scenes described. If, for instance, one describes the interaction of a mental patient with other role partners, such as a psychiatrist, a nurse, and so forth, one should write a set of instructions so that a stranger acting them out would be identified by the psychiatrist and the nurse as a mental patient—and they should behave in such a manner that the scenes described would be recreated.

To meet this criterion, one must construct "personal ideal types." The personal ideal type refers to the construction of a "puppet" endowed "with just that kind of knowledge he needs to perform the job for the sake of which he was brought into the scientific world." [10] The consciousness given to this puppet is a typification derived from the raw observation of social actors. This constructed consciousness that the observer gives to the puppet must meet the criterion of relevance. That is, the stranger following the model of the personal ideal type behaving in typical situations would be adjudged by social actors as behaving appropriately. The model, then, of an ethnographic description is this: "If a person is in situation X, performance Y [the result of following a set of instructions derived from a description] will be judged appropriate by native actors." [11] While such descriptions (and their reproducability) are not always possible, they represent an ideal for which the sociologist should strive.

Having completed his description, the sociologist has presented

9. Ward H. Goodenough, "Cultural Anthropology and Linguistics," in Dell Hymes (Ed.), *Language in Culture and Society* (New York: Harper and Row, 1964), p. 36.
10. Alfred Schutz, "The Problem of Rationality in the Social World," in A. Brodersen (Ed.), *Collected Papers* (The Hague: Martinus Nijhoff, 1964), p. 83.
11. Charles O. Frake, "Notes on Queries in Ethnography," *American Anthropologist*, Part 2, 66 (June 1964), p. 133.

a document that can be used by others for a variety of different purposes. Besides this obligation to give an adequate description, the sociologist must also attempt to identify and locate generic social patterns. Unlike the presentation of an adequate description, this is a creative act and can neither be taught nor expected to emerge from every description.

When a generic social pattern is located, it constitutes a separate subject of investigation. A study by Goffman provides one well-known example of what I have in mind. After spending a year of sociological investigation at a mental hospital and writing on its "underlife," Goffman presumably sifted through his data and emerged with the notion of "total institution" as a possible generic pattern.[12] Then, using total institution as a sensitizing concept, he showed how other organizations having diverse goals —such as military basic training camps and convents—had a similarity of behavior because of the similarity of social structure.

To illustrate further, let me mention briefly an interesting horse racing figure who will be discussed later in greater detail: namely, the "pro" who, on a day-to-day basis, successfully beats the game. What kind of information does the pro require to place successful bets, and how does he secure it? The pro, it turns out, must understand the methods of the trainer, who has a significant role in terms of the gambler's ability to beat the races. The pro must understand the trainer's long-term interests and the advantages that accrue to him from losing as well as from winning races. The trainer—as the professional race track gambler comes to understand him—has much to gain by masking his intentions with a given horse until post time. Therefore, a pro must have more than knowledge of the horse's capacity and past record, of the quality of the jockey, and the nature of the competition. Once the pro has "doped out" a winner on the basis of the above factors, he needs access to the *intentions* of the trainer.

The trainer must give final instructions to his jockey, either not to press the horse if he does not expect or desire to win, or not to spare the whip if he is going all out to win. These last-

12. Erving Goffman, *Asylums* (Chicago: Aldine Publishing Company, 1962).

minute instructions are given just before the race in a saddling
enclosure known as the "paddock." Thus, in the paddock the
trainer can no longer conceal his intentions, because his intentions must be communicated to the jockey. While the trainer can—
and does—until the paddock mobilize and direct the activities of
his stable without disclosing his intentions, the point is now
reached where disclosure becomes necessary for success.

Knowing this, the pro can capitalize upon the fact that the
paddock is in open sight of the players at the track. By observing
the trainer in interaction with the jockey—and by coming to
"know" trainers over the course of time—the pro can read cues
that will provide him with decisive betting information. The
pro looks for various idiosyncracies—whether the trainer brings
his wife or girl friend, whether or not he gives the jockey a
ticket on the horse, and so forth—for a tipoff as to the trainer's
intentions.

Note that in this example the research worker has come to
view the world of the race track through the eyes of the pro,
but not in any vague "subjective" way. The pro is viewed as a
person who pursues methods of achieving a payoff, and also as a
social actor for whom the "effective structure" of the track (that
is, "the way it works") is vitally important. Thus, by beginning
with the professional gambler, the investigator "reaches out" in
the course of his study to include jockeys, trainers, stable boys,
etc., but in a *structured* fashion. According to what I said earlier
about adequacy of description, the sociologist ought to be in a
position now to program the activities of the professional gambler
—that is, furnish a set of instructions whereby actors bring about
events. If following the rules brings about the event in a
recognizable fashion, the program has furnished an adequate
description.

As I pointed out, the sociologist must seek the widest possible
generalizations from his data. This means he must be sensitive
to the idea that his description of a scene might be but an
instance of a generic social pattern. When this is done, early
discoveries can become sensitizers and guides to later field work
in diverse situations.

To illustrate this point, let me return to what I said about the paddock. The paddock is the ecological area where an individual's intentions must take shape in action, where an individual can no longer fake his behavior, where intentions can be gleaned. From a sociological perspective, the paddock represents that point where ordinary vigilance in role deception cannot be sustained. We can move from this to looking for structurally similar situations: that of the spy, trying to ascertain the policy intentions of the enemy nation; that of the regulatory agency, probing the front activities of organizations to find out what "really is going on."

The paddock, then, is a possible feature of all organizations. Where is the paddock in a university? In a hospital? In a nation? One finds out if an enemy country is preparing for war not by reading its newspapers, but by seeing if its munitions factories are keeping their lights on late at night.

As a sensitizing concept, the "paddock" might prove useful to sociologists seeking to maximize information about an organization.

In the pages that follow, I have kept close to the phenomenological world, for my aim is primarily descriptive. While the theoretical model of the game informs the observations presented here, the overall organizing framework utilizes a dramaturgical analogy. This study is divided into three major parts: in the first I deal with the *performers*, in the second with the *audience*, and, finally, in the third with the *stage managers*, who permit interaction between performers and audience to run smoothly.

I

the

performers

2.

WHAT IS A HORSE?

Not every animal that races at the track is a horse. What is a "horse" depends upon one's point of view.

Technically, a horse is a full (ungelded) male 5 years old or older. But from the standpoint of the player, a horse is an animal that runs "hard"—regardless of age and sex. The other animals are "pigs," "dogs," "beetles," or "goats." What makes a horse a "horse" is *heart*. According to this criterion, to be a horse—as fans put it—"he's gotta have heart." We will return to this point shortly.

From the viewpoint of the breeder, a horse is a thoroughbred. But this also is a question of cultural definition. "Thoroughbred" is an American term, originating in the eighteenth century to refer to stallions imported from England. But the English distinguish a horse that races from a race horse. Most American "thoroughbreds"—the English contend—are half breds, and thus not really race horses. (In 1913, the English Jockey Club declared that a thoroughbred was henceforth defined as one that can trace both sire's and dam's side of its pedigree to horses and mares that appear in the 1791 volumes of the English General Stud Book.)

To be an American thoroughbred, a horse must be listed in the American Stud Book, first published in 1868; to be registered as a thoroughbred in the American book, a horse must be able to trace his ancestors for at least six generations of sires and five

13

of dams who have been so registered. To get listed in the American Stud Book, a horse must be registered with the Jockey Club. (This is the primary job of the Jockey Club.) No horse can be run unless registered.

In submitting his application, the owner presents four possible names for the horse. (A name cannot have more than sixteen letters, including spaces.) Members of the club frequently reject all suggested names. No name is accepted that has been used during the fifteen previous years. In addition, names of living persons are not usually eligible. Also the name of a horse considered to be one of the "immortals" cannot be used. But what is an immortal is also a decision to be made by the Jockey Club.

Besides a name, all thoroughbreds must have a number. This number is tattooed on the animal's upper lip. Lip-tattooing assures positive identifications; it is the best defense against the "ringer"—a good horse run in place of a poorer one that he is disguised to resemble. Since the betting odds on an animal will reflect his record, the horse with the poor record, if it wins, will have a big payoff. In the past, betting coups were easily arranged by a mere shuffle of a horse's cards of identity. But in 1946, lip-tattooing became a mandatory feature of racing. Such modern methods of identification have virtually eliminated ringers.

Just as every animal that races on the track with four legs is not a "horse," not every race is just a "race." For the player, a race is a "race" only when some of the animals are so evenly matched that at the finish four or five horses can be "covered by a blanket." The expression, "that's what makes a horse race," refers to a state of affairs where the individuals making estimates of the outcome of the event all have good reasons for their selections. The more horses that have a perceived possibility of winning, the closer the event comes to being a "race." Fans designate other types of races as "dog races," "goat races," or "pig races." These are races where none of the horses are viewed as having objective possibilities of winning. Where one horse stands out, the race is called a "boat race," "walk away," or "no-contest" affair. Such races are equally unpopular with the fans.

More formally, races are classified as claiming and nonclaim-

ing races. By far the greatest number of races—some 75 per cent
—are claiming races. In a claiming race, each horse is in a sense
up for sale. That is, any owner who has raced a horse at the
track during the meet in progress may put in a claim to buy any
horse racing in a claiming race. In $2,000 claiming races, any
horse can be bought for $2,000; in $5,000 claiming races, $5,000,
and so on.[1] Before the race, the person wishing to make a claim
fills out a form and presents it to one of the officials, designating
his intention to claim a certain animal. He must accompany this
with cash or a certified check. If more than one owner submits
an intention-to-claim, dice are thrown to determine who gets the
horse. As soon as the horses step onto the track for the race,
the claimed horse belongs to the new owner, though any part of
the purse the horse wins goes to the former owner. If the horse
should die on the track, the new owner must pay for carting away
the animal.

Nonclaiming races are of three general kinds: allowances,
stakes, and handicaps. Allowance races are for horses that owners
feel are too good to run in the ranks of claiming races and perhaps not good enough for stakes or handicap races. That at least
is the players' meaning. For the track officials, particularly the
track secretary who writes the conditions for all the races at a
given track, these races refer to the manner in which weight is
handled. In allowance races, the conditions for entering a horse
specify a certain base weight the eligible horses carry, with a re-
duction of a definite number of pounds for inferior prior performance (in terms of the amount of money earned or races won).
Additional weight is assigned for previous superior performance.
Here is an example of conditions for an allowance race (at a
middle-grade track) :

> Purse $3,100. For Three-Year-olds and upward. Non-winners
> of a race other than claiming at one mile or over since
> June 5. Three-year-olds, 119 lbs; older, 126 lbs. Non-winners
> of $6,500 since June 5 allowed 3 pounds; of $1,950 three

1. Virtually all claiming races in the United States range in price from
$1,000 to $20,000. The grade of a race track may be estimated by its
lowest claiming price. A high-grade track is one where the lowest claiming price is $3,000; a middle-grade track, $2,000; a low-grade track, $1,000.

times since May 8 or $5,000 since April 2, 5 lbs.; of $1,950
since July 17 or $1,885 twice since May 8, 7 lbs.; a race
of any value since May 8, 9 lbs. (Claiming races not
considered.)

In handicap races, the track handicapper assigns weights in
such a manner that all the entrants are equalized.[2] The heaviest
weighted horse is the one he considers the best; the lightest
weighted, the poorest horse. The weights will range anywhere
from 95 to 136 pounds. If a horse is assigned 120 pounds and
the jockey weighs 110, then 10 pounds of "dead weight" in the
form of lead plates are placed under the saddle. Handicap races
offer large purses (typically ranging from $10,000 to $100,000).
There is usually no more than one handicap race a week at any
given track.

The third major division of nonclaiming races are stakes races.
In a stakes race, all the entrants carry the same weight, except for
a sex allowance. When females run against males, they are given
a five-pound allowance before September and a three-pound allowance after that. (This is automatically granted and not stated
in the conditions of a race.) Stakes races are usually for 2- or
3-year-olds.

A stakes race always requires an entrance fee. The owner, to
enter a horse in a stakes race, must notify his intention well in
advance of the race and pay an initial fee. Additional fees are
paid according to a schedule to keep his nomination active. There
is also a starting fee ranging from $200 to $1,000 or more. The
track then puts up an additional sum known as "added money."
The total pot goes to the first four horses. The best known stakes
race is the Kentucky Derby.

Trainers' and jockeys' strategies differ in the two kinds of
races. In handicap races, the strategy must be such that the horse
that wins does not look too good or win by too much; otherwise
the animal will be penalized with extra poundage in his next start.

2. In his effort to equalize the horses, the track handicapper employs
"the scale of weights." Developed as a result of generations of trial and
error, the scale of weights serves as a baseline for equalizing horses of
different age and sex in competition. The base-line weights differ depending on the month and the distance of the race.

In stakes races, because the horses carry the same weight and cannot be penalized for a winning effort, true form can be exposed. The techniques and strategies of concealing form in handicap races are part of what I call information control, and will be discussed later.

When horses fail to run well in stakes, handicap, or allowance races they are put in claiming races where their chances of winning are more realistic.

A residual type of race is known as a maiden race. A "maiden" is a horse that has never won a race. On any given day, at least one race will be slated for maidens, which may be run under claiming or nonclaiming conditions. When a horse wins his first race, he is said to "break" his maiden. Tradition dictates that on such an occasion his handlers honor him with an extra helping of carrots.

Most trainers have in their barn only claiming horses, and their working categorization of types of races is based wholly upon (1) levels of claiming price, (2) races for age and sex, and (3) distance. Distances are designated as either "sprints" or "routes." Sprint races are from two furlongs to seven furlongs. (A furlong is one-eighth of a mile.) Route races are from one mile to two miles. The most frequently run distance is that of six furlongs. Very few horses can perform well at all distances. Horses that can run well at six furlongs will consistently be beaten at one mile. At times, trainers will place a horse in races at a distance that is unfavorable for the horse to disguise his true form. More about that later.

Age and sex designations are important because horsemen are not free to enter just any horse in any race. Many conditions state "for fillies and mares only," or "for 3-year-olds only," "for 2-year-old fillies," and so forth. Females are never denied an opportunity to run against males. Horsemen in general believe that females cannot beat males even with the weight-sex allowance.

HEART, CLASS, AND HONOR

Heart is the perceived quality of always trying and succeeding against formidable obstacles. Thus when an animal has won a handicap race, horsemen are not concerned with the time of the race, but how much weight he carried. To win with the obstacle of weight is to demonstrate the quality that horsemen have in mind when they talk about improving the breed.

The ultimate display of heart is to die in the cause of victory. Here is an eyewitness account of a crowd's reaction to a horse that won by a nose and then dropped dead after passing the finish line:

> That was a heartless crowd, as track crowds go. It wasn't much of a bunch for sentiment. And it was cold and snowing and dark and damp. The people were keen to take the train back to warm Washington. But they didn't rush for it as they ordinarily would. They gathered around the dead wreck of a horse, picked him up and carried him to a spot just outside the paddock. On the field of honor, they dug a grave and buried him.[3]

The opposite of heart, as horsemen put it, is "chicken shit." Two other terms used to designate the horse without heart are "quitter" and "morning glory." The morning glory is a horse that burns up the track in his morning workouts, but fails to perform in the heat of competition. The quitter is a horse that takes the lead in a race and stops when headed by another horse. Gray horses are often stigmatized as "quitters." The theory that gray horses quit is fulfilled by a self-confirming hypothesis. Because grays are thought to quit, they are frequently trained to run in front where hopefully they won't be running head and head with the competition. Now any horse will quit when pressed on a fast pace. Since so many grays are trained to run in front and since in almost every race there is at least one horse that will press the horse on the lead, the gray in front will often stop from sheer

3. Winnie O'Connor, *Jockeys, Crooks and Kings* (New York: Jonathan Cape and Harrison Smith, 1930), pp. 39–40.

exhaustion. But because of the lay theory that grays quit, the gray is *perceived* as quitting. In turn, this is taken as evidence to support the theory.

A lay concept related to heart is "class." Class is measured by comparative dominance. When other factors—the condition of the animal, the distance of the race, weights—are held constant, class is said to always determine the outcome of an event. To say that Horse A has more class than Horse B means that A can defeat B. In baseball, if team A beats team B, and team B beats C, it still remains problematic that team A will beat team C. Now if we substitute horses for baseball teams, the outcome is held to be nonproblematic. That is, if horse A has demonstrated his domi- nance over horse B, and if horse B has demonstrated his domi- nance over horse C, then horse A (other factors held more or less constant) can always be counted on to beat C. The reason given for the certainty of the outcome is class. As horsemen put it, "Class will tell."

In determining class, speed (that is, the time it takes a horse to run a certain distance) is relatively unimportant. To illustrate the point, consider a horse that typically runs in $4,000 claiming races. On a winning day, he may run six furlongs in 1:10 (read, one minute and ten seconds). A week later, if entered against $5,000 claimers, he can be expected to bring up the rear of the field far behind the winner, although the final time may be 1:11. (A second is equivalent to five lengths, a length being the measure of a horse from head to tail.) The reverse of this situation is also a frequent occurrence. Consider, for instance, a horse that con- sistently fails to win in $5,000 claiming races, though the final time of these races may be a relatively slow 1:12. When dropped into a claiming race for $4,000, he will often win running the six- furlong distance in faster time than was recorded by the winners of the higher-grade animals against which he lost. In other words, a particular horse will be consistently beaten by higher-grade horses that run in 1:12, but the same horse will consistently beat lower-grade horses running the distance in 1:10. This phenomenon is regarded as one of the strangest characteristics of thoroughbreds.

Horsemen explain this phenomenon by viewing class as the

ability of a horse to look another in the eye and run the other
into the ground. This is the horsemen's version of the pecking-order
phenomenon. Class, then, is conceived as the comparative dominance of horses: *a horse with higher class will run as fast as necessary to beat a horse with lower class.* The reason this does not
happen every time is because of those factors that are not equal,
such as the amount of weight that a horse carries.

To horsemen and players, there is no necessary relation between class and heart. In fact, heart is always measured in terms
of the horse's presumed class. If an animal of $4,000 class runs
hard and demonstrates courage when entered in a race against
$4,000 horses, he is considered an animal with heart. If he is
placed in a race with $6,500-class horses and does not show a lick
(that is, he refuses to extend himself), he would not be called
"chicken shit," for the entire affair is discounted. Thus heart is
always relative to class.

Although horsemen keep the concepts of class and heart distinct, they believe that only at the highest level of class does one
find the finest display of heart. Such a horse is accorded honor.
Honor is accorded a horse in various ways. One way is to refer
to a year as belonging to a certain horse. Among horsemen, for
example, 1941 was Whirlaway's year; 1948 was Citation's year;
and 1953 was Tom Fool's year. These years serve as benchmarks
or personal calendars for horsemen. Thus, a horseman in an auto-
biographical statement may remark: "I got married in Citation's
year," and assume that the informed listener will know he was
married in 1948.

Honor is also bestowed on a horse when he so overshadows
the competition that no betting is permitted on the race. In such
races, the horse demonstrates his worthiness of the honor by attempting to beat the track record. Since other animals are not
competitors, he competes with the impersonal physical world.

Another honor that can be accorded a horse is the "walkover"
race, where all the horses are withdrawn, leaving one horse to
walk over the distance and collect the purse. Any other horse that
competes would be given a percentage of the purse and, in a

monetary sense, the owners have everything to gain. The other horses, however, are withdrawn in part as a tribute to a great horse.

Class and heart will sometimes determine whether a horse lives or dies—or dies in disgrace or honor. For example, if a horse breaks a leg in a race, he will typically be shot or given a lethal hypodermic dose. If the horse has demonstrated class and heart, every effort will be made to spare the horse and perhaps save it for breeding. If it is a horse that has shown heart and is destroyed, it will often be given a burial and a memorial will be erected; if not, it goes to the glue factory.

Some horses are said to be royally bred, but that is not enough to be saved for stud duty. Regardless of fine breeding, a horse must survive the merit test—and this is established by displaying heart in the heat of competition. Sometimes a horse with "royal breeding" (as horsemen term it) will, because of injury, fail to race, and may be put in stud duty. But because the horse has never been put to the test and has never displayed heart, the breeder will be unable to ask for a breeding fee. Horses that have displayed heart can command a breeding fee as high as $20,000.

The horse that has shown his worth in competition and has been accorded honor is shrouded with a mystique that on the human level is referred to as charisma. Thus the Jockey Club has ruled that artificial insemination is not permissible in breeding; for it is felt that only in the actual act of mating is the charisma of the horse transmitted to its offspring.

A rich breeding folklore bordering on magical beliefs surrounds the charismatic stallion. It is often felt, for example, that the horses of highest quality are made nervous by the sex act. It is further believed that "common horses" (thoroughbreds that have failed to display heart or class) are "horny" or lustful animals, whereas the class thoroughbreds are too sensitive for horsey displays of affection. When a mare is to be serviced, her tail is bandaged up, and she is led to the stall of a horse known as a teaser. The teaser is a common horse, whose function is to try the mare to see whether she is in season. The nerves of the stallion are said to get upset if a mare is not ready and a feminine rebuff, it is believed, may lead to impotence. Breeders have a ready supply of anecdotal experiences to justify this belief.

ONSTAGE, OFFSTAGE, AND BACKSTAGE

During the running of a race, a horse is "onstage." When he becomes an object of observation to the public, he is "offstage." This means from the time he is brought into the paddock to be saddled to the time the horses leave the starting gate. The "off-stage" period lasts about twenty minutes. The "backstage" area is where the animal is rehearsed for his other stage performances.[4]

Of course, a horse can only establish heart while he is onstage. Two ways of establishing heart involve the manner in which a race is run and the amount of weight a horse carries. The latter criterion is especially relevant in handicap races, where the track secretary attempts to equalize the horses by loading down the top horse with lead. In the running of the race, the horse that goes to the front and fights off all challenges or a horse that comes from far back to overcome the opposition is said to have heart.

While onstage, a horse's perceived attempt to establish heart can be disrupted by accidents. These accidents represent a routine class of unpredictables that constitute for the audience a legitimate excuse for a poor performance. The performance, in other words, is discounted. These accidents are routine in that they constitute a recurrent and thus a "perceivedly normal"[5] part of the scene. A list of the most frequent "normal" accidents includes such occurrences as a horse being left at the gate, taking a misstep and throwing the jockey, being caught in a pocket and unable to

4. Goffman distinguishes only on stage and back stage behavior. *Presentation of Self, op. cit.,* chapter 3. The notion of "off stage" is relevant to the racing scene and perhaps in other social arenas as well.

5. The term "perceivedly normal" is used in the sense described by Harold Garfinkel. See especially "Common Sense Knowledge of Social Structures," in Jordan M. Scher (Ed.), *Theories of the Mind* (New York: Free Press of Glencoe, 1962).

find racing room, going wide and losing much ground, being bumped by another horse, and so forth. A horse meeting any of these accidents is excused in the sense that his performance need not be taken as an indicator of his class or heart. Whether any of these accidents will occur to any given horse is considered a matter of luck.

Besides these observed onstage incidents, unobserved mishaps frequently occur in the offstage area, disrupting the onstage performance. The perils along the path from the paddock to the starting gate may be as slight as the nerve-rattling sound of a track restaurant dishwasher.[6] A poor onstage performance can often be traced to such offstage happenings.

While players concentrate on the onstage performance, another audience—racing officials—is equally concerned with the offstage performance. Here, the horse that fails to meet standards of adequate performance is designated "a bad actor" (that is, a horse that forgets his lines in the offstage area). Specifically he forgets what he has learned by being temperamental, making him a problem in the paddock or at the starting gate. If a horse creates a rumpus during the prerace ritual and if he does not mend his ways, he is banned from racing. The problem of "bad acting" is most tolerated in the case of 2-year-olds, since they are just learning their lines. Still, before a 2-year-old is allowed to start in his first race, he has to be approved by the official starter during the morning "schooling" period. When older horses fail to meet the standards of starting-gate etiquette, they are placed on a "starter's list" and required to undertake further backstage rehearsals before being permitted to race again.

An onstage performance that lasts one minute might have two or more years of backstage activity to bring off the event. If, in the extreme case, a horse is being prepared to win a certain type of futurity race (a stakes race for 2-year-olds), the owner must declare his intention to enter the horse before the birth of the animal. After months of preparation in teaching a horse the rudi-

6. Ted Atkinson describes such an instance in his very useful autobiography, *All the Way* (New York: Paxton Slade, 1961), pp. 51–52.

ments of etiquette, further months are devoted to building up his wind and speed by long gallops and short trials (workouts). Bringing a horse up to a race requires delicate judgment on the part of the trainer, the man behind the horse. But success also depends—as we shall now see—on the activities of the man *on* the horse.

3.

THE MAN ON THE HORSE

CHARACTER AND COOLNESS

Worship, as Durkheim has taught us,[1] involves the collective re-affirmation of moral values. Now if we ask where the virtues of moral character—courage, integrity, dignity, and so forth—are reaffirmed in action, we arrive at a curious irony that the race track and not the church is a place of worship.

Attributes of moral character are established only in risk-taking situations: before we are ready to impute to a person the quality of strong character, he must be seen as voluntarily putting something on the line.[2]

At the race track, we find a sphere of life where men are out to establish character, demonstrate virtue, and achieve honor. These men are the jockeys; and while on stage they are putting on the line their money, their reputations, and their lives.

The jockey is one of the few survivals of the traditional concept of "the man of honor"—which interestingly has always been synonymous with "the man on the horse": *cavalier, caballero,* knight.

1. Emile Durkheim, *The Elementary Forms of Religious Life* (New York: The Free Press of Glencoe, 1957). I am indebted to Erving Goffman for the general point suggested in this paragraph.
2. This is the central point of Goffman's essay, "Where the Action Is," in *Interaction Ritual* (Chicago: Aldine Publishing Company, 1967).

Feats of gallantry—or the capacity to follow the rules of decorum when it is costly to do so—are not uncommon at the track. Thus a jockey in a neck-and-neck duel down the stretch has been known to casually hand his whip to a rider who dropped his in the course of the race—and then resume a strenuous hand ride to a winning finish, demonstrating a prideful self-confidence of succeeding though under a handicap.[3]

Integrity, another attribute of moral character, is not mere honesty, but honesty when it is costly to oneself to be honest. An illustration of what I have in mind involves the case of a leading jockey whose license was revoked for betting on mounts other than his own. A wire tap revealed that the jockey had made 27 bets *against* his own mounts; but in eleven of these races he rode the winner.[4] This case dramatically illustrates one of the stable features of horse racing: when a jockey is placed in a situation where he must choose between playing for himself or playing for some other party that employs him, he will opt for the other party. That is, he chooses integrity. Thus we can expect integrity even from a dishonest jockey.

Above all, the jockey with strong character possesses the perceived virtue of coolness. A jockey who possesses this attribute is said to always "keep his cool," "to ride like an ice man," or to have ice in his veins. The ideal horse-jockey combination is a fiery animal and an icy rider.

The cool jockey can wait patiently with a horse in a pocket and get through on the inside, risking the possibility that there will be no opening. Coolness is waiting far back in the pack, risking the possibility that his horse will not "get up" in time. Coolness is sparing the whip on a front-running horse when another animal has pressed into the lead, risking the possibility that once his horse is passed he will not get started again. All these activities are taken by observers as instances of a jockey's character. In short, moral character is coolness in risky situations.

As mentioned earlier, morning glories are horses that perform well offstage but fail to demonstrate heart in the heat of compe-

3. For an illustration see Atkinson, *op. cit.*, p. 66.
4. Tom Ainslie, *Ainslie's Jockey Book* (New York: Trident Press, 1967).

tition. The term is also used for jockeys who display all the necessary skills in the morning workouts but lack coolness in the heat of battle. Horsemen believe—no doubt expressing a stereo· typical bias—that Negroes lack the moral character necessary for being jockeys, though they are thought to possess a "sweet seat" and "strong hands." (Thus there are many Negro exercise boys, but very few Negro jockeys.) By a kind of self-fulfilling hypothe- sis, the belief is maintained. When a Negro exercise boy is given opportunities to "don the silks" in the afternoon, he tries so hard to make a good showing that as a result he shows a lack of cool- ness. Interestingly, in the nineteenth century most jockeys were Negroes, and one of the reputed all-time greats was Isaac Murphy, a Negro. Horsemen acknowledge this, but contend that the style of racing has changed in such a way that qualities are called for today that were less important in an earlier day, qualities that are captured by the term "coolness."

After a jockey has suffered a serious fall, many players feel they should avoid betting on his later mounts. They feel that he has lost his moral character. Horsemen themselves share this be- lief and are reluctant to give mounts in important races to jockeys who are making a comeback. Naturally, jockeys fear the physical consequences of a serious spill. But what is not so obvious is that they fear that a spill will cause them to lose their character; simi- larly, they fear that others will perceive them as losing their character.

What the above discussion has implied and what will now be made explicit is that traits of moral character are generated by social organization.

To begin with a jockey's success depends upon his getting mounts on winning horses. The greenest boy can outride the greatest reinsman—if the former has a superior horse. How, then, does a jockey get the best horses? Simply by having the widest selection of mounts from which to choose. What a jockey wants is a choice between several mounts in a race; he wants to be in demand. And to be in demand he must somehow mobilize his activities so as to *appear* to possess those virtues of character that horsemen deem important for jockeys—integrity, gameness, coolness. In other words, a jockey must commit himself to a line of risk-taking because not to do so would constitute an even greater loss to self.[5]

BECOMING A JOCKEY

To start his career as a jockey, a young man need only convince an employer to take him on. A boy need not ever have been on a horse so long as he meets the physical requirements of size and the psychological requirement of desire.[6]

Once employed he starts as a stable boy—carrying water, mucking stalls, polishing tack, walking hots (horses that are cooled out after working or racing). He also rides about with the horse when shipped and sleeps on straw. Trainers view these demeaning activities as a kind of initiation period. As one put it: "If a boy is willing to travel 300 miles in the back of a van sleeping on piss-soaked straw, or if he wades through a stall full of shit at 5:30 every morning for no pay, you know he wants to be a jock." These activities are known as "learning horse."

The stable boy himself does not think of these activities as particularly demeaning, so long as it is clear that they are part of the first step of his career. Some fail to get beyond the stage of stable boy and are permanently placed here; others get here as a result of downward mobility (for example, exercise boys who have gone bad). For the young man performing demeaning activities, one of the protective factors to self is age: culturally, we expect boys to engage in dirty work. To distinguish himself from the "failures," the upwardly mobile stable boy will walk about with riding boots (though he is not yet permitted to ride), and during

5. Commitment, then, involves some kind of side bet, such as one's reputation. See Howard S. Becker, "Notes on the Concept of Commitment," *American Journal of Sociology*, 66 (July 1960), pp. 32–40.

6. There is no lower age limit to begin one's career, though most boys are "brought up" (that is, taken on as an apprentice) in their teens. Some boys seek employment after they have passed the legal age when they can quit school. Since most of the boy's chores take place from 5 to 9 A.M. and again in the early evening, he may continue with his formal schooling without gross interference with his racing career.

breaks in the routine he will prominently be squeezing rubber balls (as an aid to strengthen his hands for his anticipated future role).

Eventually, the boy is tried on a horse in a workout. If the horse responds to his urging and if the boy follows instructions, he is ready for official apprenticeship. He is placed under contract and apprenticed to the employer for three to five years. The contract, formulated by the Jockey Club, is standard throughout the country. In the contract, the boy pledges to keep the employer's secrets and to obey orders given by his representative (the trainer). The employer in turn provides room and board, a small salary, and traveling expenses.

Before the boy gets a mount in a race, he will spend months exercising horses. His designation is shifted from stable boy to exercise boy, but he must continue to muck stalls, polish tack, etc. The role of exercise boy is the most prestigious role below the rank of jockey, and is thus a status alternative that cushions the loss of face suffered by a jockey who failed to make the grade.

Horsemen say that the most important reason for exercise boys failing to become jockeys, or for jockeys dropping back to become exercise boys is their inability to make the weight. The interesting question is why do they fail to make the weight?

To begin with, size (within limits) is no barrier to becoming a jockey; for though it is atypical, jockeys—including some of the leading ones—are as tall as five feet, eleven inches. While the growing boy cannot control his height, he can control weight, given the desire that he has amply demonstrated in going through the initiation period. My observations and interviews have led me to hypothesize that a boy does not first pick up weight and then have his career blocked. Rather, career opportunities first close up and then he gains weight—though lay beliefs hold the reverse to be the case.[7] The stable boy who finds himself exercising horses for a year or so without getting a mount can see the writing on the wall; the next step in the career ladder is not being opened

7. It should be emphasized that I am here presenting a tentative hypothesis. Hard data to support the hypothesis is difficult to come by. It would be necessary to obtain weights of the boys and establish correlations (in the statistical sense) between shifts in weight and career events.

for him; he sees himself as lacking the skill or character necessary
for the competitive scene. By picking up weight, he has a face-
saving device for not going on.

Another common instance of sudden weight increase is that of
the jockey recently graduated from the apprentice ranks. Until
one year from the day he has his first mount or upon winning
forty races, whichever is the longer, the apprentice jockey is given
what is called a weight allowance or "bug." A five-pound allowance means that any horse ridden by an apprentice will carry five
pounds less than that stipulated in the race conditions. As we shall
see later, horsemen are hyperconscious of weight and believe that
five pounds equal one length—the difference between victory and
defeat in most races. Thus a "bug" is likely to get many offers to
ride, and having several mounts to choose from in a race will
increase his probability of getting hot horses. Frequently the leading jockey at any given meet is a bug, not because of his skill but
because of the advantages that come with his weight allowance.
But when a jockey loses his bug, suddenly he finds few if any
mounts forthcoming. Overnight—at the loss of a bug—the jockey
who was yesterday's hottest rider is today's inexperienced kid. At
this point, the young jockey begins to pick up weight—which generally is attributed to his being a growing boy.

The acceptable weight for an exercise boy makes face-saving
easy for an erstwhile jockey. While the virtual upper limit for a
jockey is 117 pounds, exercise boys can be as heavy as 130. Thus,
if a boy weighs 120, he might be continually asked why he doesn't
lose weight and get mounts. But if he is over 120, he is considered
beyond the point of losing weight; yet he is secure in his position
as exercise boy.

If a jockey weighs more than the horse is to carry according
to the conditions of the race, the difference is known as "overweight." Bettors believe that "overweight" has a decided effect on
the performance of a horse, and information about overweight is
taken into account before a final selection is made. Before the first
post at all tracks, the overweights of all horses are announced over
the public address system. This information is repeated before
every race and is also shown in colored-chalk notations on boards

located at various places around the track. Some handicapping systems sold to the betting public have as one of the rules: eliminate all horses carrying overweight. Many horsemen share these beliefs about the adverse effects of overweight, and a trainer on some occasions may in fact seek an overweight jockey when he wants his horse to lose.

The overweight limit is five pounds. A pound or two makes a big difference in the mounts a boy can accept. If a horse is scheduled to carry 110 pounds and the jockey scheduled to ride the mount "weighs in" at 116 (his weight and saddle and other gear are included in the weighing), he will be disqualified from riding the horse. A jockey's weight is classified in the following way: a lightweight jockey weighs less than 110 pounds; a middleweight is 110 to 113; and a heavyweight weighs above 113. To lose that extra pound or so before a race, some jockeys go through the process of "wasting," which involves daily sessions in a steam cabinet or sweating between rubber sheets.

BENCHMARKS IN A RIDER'S CAREER

A jockey who wins his first race, like a horse, is said to have broken his maiden. The news of a first win is broadcast by the public address announcer, and the crowd cheers the young man; a broken maiden is also a significant item in newspaper sports pages. In the jockeys' room, the ritual is to give the boy a cold shower—with his winning silks on.

The second major event in a jockey's career is winning the first handicap or stakes race. A jockey receives 10 per cent of the purse for a winning ride. In the heavy-purse stakes and handicap races, of say $100,000, the jockey can earn about $10,000 for a minute's work. But more than money is involved. A race for the big chips poses a real test of moral character. Here coolness is considered to be more crucial than in other races. The winning of the first handicap race is a *rite de passage* where the self-image of one who possesses moral character is dramatically confirmed.

The third important event in the jockey's career is his first bad fall. The significance of this event, as already suggested, is not whether the jockey will be injured badly enough to impede his riding. More important is whether he can—psychologically—ride at all. After a bad spill, some jockeys don't "come back"; they don't feel at home any more on a horse. But to come back after a bad fall and continue to ride with the same success as before fully authenticates one as a jockey in the eyes of horsemen; he has demonstrated the moral attribute of gameness.

In interviewing jockeys (who are difficult to interview in any case, since they are instructed to maintain a distance from strangers who might be prospective conmen or fixers), the most difficult subject to get them to talk about is falls. "We never talk about those things," one rider told me. "It happens, it happens. There's nothing to talk about."

Another jockey who after a fall failed to make a comeback said: "For a while you only get pigs to ride. The trainers with hot horses ain't out to give you a break. Only the gyps like [he mentioned a certain hand-to-mouth trainer] will put you on their plugs. I'm out of the business now. Who wants to get killed riding plugs?"

Income and Expenses

Whether they ride plugs or hot mounts, jockeys' riding fees are the same. The usual guidelines, as established by the racing associations, are $20 for an unplaced horse, $25 for third, $35 for second, and $50 for first. By tradition, the winning jockey also receives 10 per cent of the purse.

Jockeys have many expenses. Except for the silks, they own everything that goes on the horse. A jockey has about $1,000 invested in his "stage clothes": boots, pants, saddles, and other tack.

A much more expensive overhead is the jockey's agent, who receives 20 per cent of the earnings—on winning or losing mounts. Jockeys typically do not resent such fees; most believe that their success or failure on the turf depends as much on the agent as anything else. Only occasionally does a jockey refer to his agent as "my pimp." The agent's job is to solicit mounts for the rider. If the boy is hot, the agent has no problem and may insist that a trainer wanting the jockey's services pay a flat fee, usually 10 per cent of the purse, win or lose. Usually handling only one jockey, the agent closely identifies with his boy. When discussing the successes or failures of his boy, an agent often refers to him as "I" [8] —"I'm getting nothing to ride these days but cripples," "I was just nosed out on three mounts yesterday," etc.

One aspect of the agent's role is to cool out the losing jockey. When a jockey loses on a favorite, the agent will say that the horse shouldn't have been a favorite; for it wasn't the best horse in the race. If the jockey falls into a slump, the agent will point out the names of all the jockeys who are in a slump, recall the time that some leading jockey had 52 consecutive losers, and expound on a philosophy that deals with the swinging pendulum of luck.

Typically, jockeys don't enter into contracts with agents. The arrangement is based on common understandings. Some jockeys change agents frequently, especially when in a slump, or when they believe that the agent isn't getting enough good mounts. Some agents will go to great lengths to get mounts for their boys, at times going so far as to exercise horses free to establish a relation of indebtedness with trainers. The success of an agent can easily be determined by his demeanor. The agent with the hot boy is quiet, tight-lipped, and noncommittal. The struggling agent is a friendly hail-fellow well met, ready to slap a trainer on the back and offer him a favor. Unless one is aware of the structural elements that determine the agents' "personalities," one might conclude—in observing the same agents over a period of years—that they are a manic-depressive breed.

The jockey's other expense is the valet. The valet is employed by the track, but receives about $5 a mount and $10 a winner from the jockey. At getaway day (that is, the last day of a meet), the jockey customarily gives his valet a bonus of $100 or more, depending on his success. The valets are frequently former jockeys

8. Ainslie, *op. cit.*, p. 6.

who have grown too big, too old, or too inept to continue as riders. The valets are treated with a good deal of charity; many jockeys feel that "there but for the grace of God. . . ."

About twenty minutes before post time, the jockeys are weighed for the race in the scale room, and the clerk checks the reading against the assigned weight. If the jockey is light, the clerk will tell the valet, "Give him a shade," and if the boy is heavy, the clerk may suggest, "Try a lighter saddle pad." [9]

After being fitted out at the proper weight, the jockey hands his equipment to a valet who goes to the paddock where he assists the trainer in saddling the horse. Later, when the jockey has weighed in after the race, the valet takes his equipment and returns it to the jockeys' quarters. In his free time, the valet looks after the tack, arranges clothes, helps the jockey dress, etc.

TYPES OF JOCKEYS

Horsemen recognize three categories of jockeys: "honest boys," "money jocks," and "businessmen."

To get the reputation of an honest boy (most jockeys are so categorized) a jockey must satisfy two conditions: he must accept all mounts offered him, and he must ride in strict accord to instructions.

If a jockey's services are called upon, he must not refuse, lest his reputation as "honest" be damaged. The only legitimate reason for not accepting a mount is to have already accepted a bid to ride some other trainer's horse. Given this cultural expectation, we might expect that all trainers would freely attempt to gain the services of the hottest jockeys, ensuring the best possible chance of their horses finishing in the money. Moreover, we might expect that given a choice between mounts, the jockeys will always choose the hot horse. In actuality, trainers will often call upon second-rate jockeys to ride their horses; and jockeys will often choose to ride a second-rate horse. These anomalous choices deserve some explanation.

9. Atkinson, *op cit.*, p. 171.

When a trainer has a horse whose expected performance for a particular event is highly uncertain, often he will prefer to call upon the services of a lesser known jockey. Should he choose a superior jockey and should the horse perform very poorly, then the superior jockey will—when given a choice in the future—choose to ride for another trainer. The trainer's disinclination to ask a hot jockey to ride an uncertain animal has the consequence of resolving the jockey's dilemma: to be "honest" he must accept all mounts—usually on a first-come, first-served basis—but to maintain a good winning record he needs a choice from among *hot* mounts. In sum, trainers in the pursuit of their own self-interest help jockeys maintain their reputation as being both "honest" and "hot."

From time to time, however, a trainer will call upon the services of a hot boy even when he knows for certain that his animal will do little running on a particular day. In the erratic horse's next race, where the winning effort is planned, the trainer may shift to a no-name jockey. This shifting from a hot jockey to a no-name boy is a maneuver to get better odds. The playing public reasons this way: "If hot jock Jones can't bring the animal home, the horse is a nothing." When the horse wins next time at a big price with the no-name jock, the public attributes the victory to some factor of racing luck and not to the manipulations of the man behind the horse. Naturally, the trainer can't pull this maneuver too often, for fear of alienating a good jockey. Moreover, each time the trainer employs this maneuver, he is tacitly indebted to "pay off" the jockey by furnishing him with a hot mount in the future.

As I have already suggested, the hot jock will sometimes choose to ride what he takes to be an inferior mount. Such decisions typically involve horses from the leading money-winning stables. The jockey "trades" a bad mount today for a good mount tomorrow. That is, the winning stable, when it has a hot horse, will go back with the boy who is willing to ride those horses whose performance is uncertain.

In general, a type of equilibrium is established whereby the leading trainers get the leading jocks to ride for them, and the

leading jocks get the best mounts. But, as I indicated, this state
of affairs is the result of many sorts of exchanges and tacit
negotiations.

The second criterion of a jock's reputation as "honest"—
strictly following instructions of the trainer—can be explained
more briefly. Trainers, for reasons that will be made clear later,
often have something to gain when their horses lose on a particular occasion. One way of making a horse lose or appear to be
off form is to instruct the jockey to run the animal in a manner
contrary to the horse's best efforts. If a horse runs best in front,
the trainer who wants to lose will instruct the jockey to come
from behind; if the horse runs best close to the rail, the trainer
will instruct the jockey to keep the horse wide; if the horse responds only to energetic whipping, the trainer will instruct the
jockey not to use the whip. The jockey may well realize that the
instructions are contrary to the horse's best efforts; he might
realize that by *not* following instructions he can win an otherwise
losing race. However, he will *not* race in accord with his own best
judgment, because what he has at stake is his reputation as an
"honest boy."

The second type of jockey—the "money jock"—is not concerned with the number of mounts he receives but with getting
the best mounts in the best races. If he had his way, the money
jock would accept only mounts in the feature Saturday race. In
receiving mounts, his agent is often instructed to demand a flat fee
for his services. For instance, the stable demanding the services
of the money jock must meet a set fee of, say, $250 (10 per cent
of the winning share in most ordinary races) on a win-or-lose
basis. This demand usually means that the jock will get hot
mounts, for owners are slow to put up a win-or-lose fee unless they
have a hot horse and expect to win. By getting hot horses, the
money jock will be on a mount where he can display his skills and
character to best advantage. These are some of the backstage
manipulations that make his onstage performance appear so
stunning.

Money jocks are preferred by moneyed stables. The leading
handicap and stakes horses are to be found in the barns of those

owners who regard horse racing literally as a game. Being able to foot the bills, their concern is with the honor that goes with owning (and frequently breeding) the *winner*. Second- or third-place money is seldom a target for these owners.

The characteristic of the money jock is his in-and-out performance. When he is "in," it is frequently because he has—as a consequence of his coolness—staged a ride that saved the horse perhaps as much as five lengths. Many horsemen say that a money jock can give a horse a five-length advantage. They believe the money jock can remain cool in a pocket and plunge through on the inside rail when and if the opportunity comes, rather than taking a horse on the outside where the certainty of racing room may cost a horse five lengths. Since one length equals five pounds (by rule of thumb calculation accepted by racing secretaries), the right kind of ride can—in lay theory at least—make up for a deficit of 25 pounds spotted to the opposition. In short, the moneyed stables depend on the money jocks to bring home *first* money.

The third type of jockey—the "businessman"—is a boy who "gets what he can, any way he can," as one observer put it. This is the lay image most spectators have of all jockeys. Even Devereux, in his study of gambling, suggests that because the jockey's racing days are numbered, he will be inclined to conspire with gamblers in their betting coups. By entering into the plans of gamblers by, let us say, pulling a horse on orders (presumably to protect the bookies against a large loss), the jockey can solidify his relations with the gamblers who may be of help to him after retirement.[10]

Devereux's remarks represent an interesting theory of an activity that occurred in a real *past* or a *fictionalized* present. To begin with, jockeys—unlike most other athletes—are neither limited as to age nor do they believe they are. Unlike boxers, baseball players, and football pros who are called old men at 35 and are retired by 40, jockeys have been active and in fact won some of the richest handicap races while in their late fifties; two of the most prominent boys (jockeys are boys at any age) were Pat Remmilard and Johnny Longden, both of whom were racing until their

10. Devereux, *op. cit.*, p. 424.

sixtieth years. Asked when jockeys should retire, they respond not by mentioning an age, but say, "When you can't get any more mounts." Second, retirement funds and pension plans (for jockeys disabled in a spill) cushion the pressure of "getting it" while you can. Finally, and most important, the surveillance system (discussed later) of the various racing associations and the severity of sanctions (being ruled off the turf for misconduct) virtually have done away with the "businessman" who has conspired with gamblers to fix a race.

As the term is used today, "businessman" refers to the type of jockey whose overwhelming motivation is the profit motive. This motive is expressed in the jock's assertion, heard in the business world but seldom among the other jocks, "I'm not in business for my health." Further, businessmen believe that, at least for them, the way to make money is by betting on their mounts. So far as possible, businessmen will seek mounts on horses they think are ready to win at a good price.

Among those jockeys who have no agents, by far the largest group are the businessmen. Preferring to hustle their own mounts, they seek out the small-time owner-trainer who stables "platers" (cheap claiming horses). This type of trainer can't pay the win-or-lose fee demanded by the money jocks, nor does he expect to get the hot jocks who are cultivating greener pastures. A more likely choice of rider is the businessman. Moreover, since the owner-trainer has to foot all the bills, he finds in the businessman an opportunity to cut corners. Frequently the businessman will exercise horses free or simply wait for payment until the stable is having some success. In exchange, the owner-trainer takes the jockey into his confidence and strategies are worked out together. Although not under contract to the owner-trainer, the jock often will travel the various circuits with him.

The owner-trainer with whom the businessman associates is invariably one who doesn't bet and often has the reputation of being poor but honest. This sets the stage for a mutually advantageous arrangement. A betting trainer would take great pains to conceal his intentions and limit the information flow; for a leak of intentions would affect the odds on the horse, and he wishes to get the most for his betting investment. Since the nonbetting trainer has little to lose by revealing his intentions to a jockey (even the nonbetting trainer has *something* to lose by revealing information about his horse, especially in claiming races, as we shall later see), he can get the services of a skillful jockey for little cost: namely, information concerning his intentions.

The businessman is quick to see the advantage in hooking up with the honest trainer. A brief explanation of the problems of putting over a coup will show why this is the case. When betting trainers manipulate horses for the purpose of winning bets, the investigative activities of the racing association quickly get wind of this and place pressure on the stable (just what pressures can be applied will be discussed later). To avoid such investigations, betting stables today engage in *partial* concealment of a horse's true form. A partial concealment, however, implies a partial disclosure of form, which legitimates a horse's winning (that is, nothing is incongruous about a horse winning if it has displayed a recent fair effort). On the other hand, the fact that form has been partly concealed helps assure a fair price (conceived typically at odds of about 4 to 1). Betting stables do not run "in-and-outers" or "sharp wakeups" that pay "boxcar mutuels" (winners with very big payoffs). Thus the gambling stables work to maintain the impression of simon-pure honesty. The known nonbetting, honest trainer, however, can run hot-and-cold horses and win at boxcar mutuels with impunity; officials will take for granted that the erratic performance of his horses is due to low-grade stock, thought to be naturally unpredictable. Also as long as the boxcar mutuels are coming from the horses of honest stables, in-and-out performances are tolerated—indeed, welcome—for they give variety in the payoffs. To the businessman jockey, one or two bets on one or two 40-to-1 shots during a 55-day racing meet are big dividends. Thus the betting jockey prefers to stick with the honest trainer. Indirectly, then, in the manner I have suggested, honesty is in the service of "vice."

When two or three businessmen are in the same race, the scene is set for possible chicanery. One may find here the closest thing to a fixed race, what is called a "jockeys' race." Here two

or three boys, surveying the situation in the jocks' room before
going to the paddock, will come to an understanding through a
kind of tacit bargaining. The conversation among businessmen
Tom, Dick, and Harry might run something like this:

Tom: How do you like your mounts today, fellers?

Dick: Well, I have a ready horse, but I'm not going to bet a
dime. There's nothing that will keep up with the favorite.

Harry: My horse is pretty fair, too, but no use killing him
for show dough. He'll be saved for next week. Think I'll bet
him then.

Tom: You know, guys, my horse can turn it on in the
stretch. If only something would go with the favorite for a
mile and knock the wind out of him! You know, Dick, if
your horse went with the favorite for half a mile and then
you, Harry, picked him up at the far turn, the favorite
would be a dead duck. And if I can get home with Slow
Bones, I'll be glad to "save" with you boys.

That is all that need be said. The favorite is knocked out of
competition by the top of the stretch, and Tom waltzes home on
Slow Bones at 20 to 1. Next time, perhaps it will be Harry's
turn to come home first.

A jockeys' race—when it occurs at all—takes place in the last
race. One reason for this is that the cheapest race of the day is
typically the last race, and here we would be more likely to find
two or three businessmen in the same race. Second, the last race
is almost always a distance race, at least $1 \frac{1}{16}$ miles. The longer
distance is necessary for working out a strategy (however vaguely
suggested). In a sprint race most of the horses are rushing from
start to finish, and strategies to control the pace of the race are
not easy to put into operation (unless the planning is highly
deliberate and carefully worked out). The most important feature
of the last race is that it is the *last* race. At this time the stewards
tend to relax their usual vigilance, and the crowd is dispersing
and is less likely to shout disapproval at what appears to be a

jockeys' race. In fact, many fans assume that the last race will be a jockeys' race and will be stabbing for a long shot to get even on the assumption that a long shot has a better chance in the last race than it would otherwise. And when a long shot does suddenly pop home a winner the crowd—even when they haven't bet on the particular horse—voices a kind of approval. On homeward-bound buses and trains, the conversation will center on how the player bet or almost bet the winning long shot in the last race. On the other hand, a favored horse winning the last race is unpopular; the mass of players are betting long shots to get even. A subtle pressure is exerted on the stewards not to inquire too closely into the last race, since one of their jobs is to keep the public content. A jockey's race sometimes gives the appearance of a well-rehearsed performance, and yet there is nothing specific to put one's finger on. Nothing is, strictly speaking, illegal.

Another feature of the last race is that the riders, often having only one mount that day, have been sitting in the jockeys' room together for six hours, and as time has passed, eventually have turned their conversation to the race they will run. According to the rules of racing, the jockey—even if he has only one mount—must report to the jockeys' room one hour before the first race, and remain there until riding his last mount of the day. The sheer amount of time jockeys spend together is conducive to "discussing things."

Finally, the businessman is generally better informed than any other type of jockey about the condition of the animal he is to ride and the intentions of the stable. Moreover, since the businessman often has the trainer in his debt, he can get away with not running the race exactly to orders, which in any case will be something like: "You know what the horse can do. Just do your best."

The businessman jockey doesn't see anything wrong with the staging of a race and would probably be mildly shocked if accused of dishonest dealings. The cooperative arrangement is viewed as just another version of the traditional practice of "saving." During a race, a rider may try to make a bargain to share the purse. For instance, two horses may enter the stretch head and head, and one jock will call out: "How about saving?" The other might say: "You're on."

Although the practice of saving is frowned upon officially in most races, it is a mandatory practice among jockeys who ride as an entry in a stakes or handicap race. For example, a stable might enter two (or more) horses in a race, and the jockeys arrange a 60–40 split if one should win.

The bargaining arrangement that occurs among businessmen is to them but a form of the legitimate practice of saving. They legitimate the arrangements they make by referring to it as saving, just as trusted bank employees justify their embezzlement by referring to it as "borrowing." [11]

In sum, an analysis of the deviant practice of the jockeys' race involves the conditions typically thought to be relevant in the analysis of most kinds of deviance.[12] First the *conduciveness* and *opportunity* associated with knowing something about the trainer's intentions and being thrown into interaction together permitting the teaming up in a deviant act; the *strain* placed on the businessman who wins only a few races and has relatively few mounts and must make these count; the *legitimation* of the course of action through a "neutralization technique" [13] of saving; and finally, a *laxity of social control*—characteristic of the last race milieu—on the part of the racing officials.[14]

COMMUNICATION STRATEGIES

During a race, the jockeys must keep in mind three separate audiences—the fans, the horsemen and the officials—each of

11. Donald Cressey, *Other Peoples' Money* (New York: The Free Press of Glencoe, 1953).

12. Albert K. Cohen, "The Sociology of the Deviant Act," *American Sociological Review*, 30 (February 1965), pp. 9–14.

13. Gresham M. Sykes and David Matza, "Techniques of Neutralization," *American Sociological Review*, 22 (December 1957), pp. 667–669.

14. Taken together, these components of a deviant act constitute what Smelser, *op. cit.*, calls a value-added process, which he uses in his explanatory model of all kinds of collective behavior.

which is demanding a certain kind of performance. The crowd wants an energetic effort; the officials, an honest, free-from-fouling ride; the trainer, a ride to orders. These different audiences frequently make demands at cross purposes. The trainer may instruct the jockey not to press the horse, and this may appear to the crowd as the absence of an energetic ride; and if the horse is heavily bet on, the jockey might be booed. On the other hand, the trainer may give the jockey instructions to get out in front at once, which often involves cutting across the field rapidly and may lead to officials' sanctioning for rough-riding.

Whatever the orders, the jockey must at least *appear* to be riding energetically and cleanly. To bring off these appearances the jockey has developed certain communication strategies—*dramatic accentuation* and *concealment* or a combination of both. (Thus the jockey engages in impression management even in situations of total involvement.)

Dramatic accentuation refers to the exaggeration of an aspect of one's performance. Horsemen sometimes speak of this strategy as riding in the style of Don Meade. In 1930, Don Meade was ruled off the turf for betting on horses other than his own. After several years of applying to be reinstated, he was finally given a license to ride on the strength of a promise that "if they just give me one more chance, they'll see a jockey ride as none had ever ridden in history." To keep his promise he dramatically accentuated an always-trying riding style. "Stigmatized as a jockey who would throw a race, he always pushed his mounts to their utmost, and made a display of this that became part of his characteristic riding style—of shoving a horse. . . ." [15] Today jockeys who think they are under suspicion suddenly adopt the Meade style. To some degree, all jockeys adopt this style to appear honest and energetic. This style, emphasizing the energetic use of hands and legs, does not improve the horse's performance. It is all part of impression management.

Oddly enough, this strategy not only takes in the audience of fans, but also the other jockeys. Some jockeys become specialists

15. Charles B. Parmer, *For Gold and Glory* (New York: Carrick and Evans, 1939), p. 212.

in appearing to be working so hard on a horse that the other jockeys in a race may assume that the horse being worked on is tiring fast. The jockey on a front-running mount may begin to wave his elbows furiously (known as "pumping"), and the other jockeys, believing that the horse will soon slow up, will wait before making a move. Suddenly, just as the horse appears to be finished and the other horses make their move, the front horse jumps out to a bigger lead and now is really being pressed by its jockey for the first time. Even when the other jockeys suspect that pumping may be a deception, they can never be sure. Hence, at the very least, the strategy undercuts certainty. While pumping can be used as a strategy to win a race, it is equally serviceable for the jock who has instructions to lose a race. He can save a horse for another race and at the same time give the appearance to the fans and officials of pressing hard.

The example of pumping illustrates that techniques of dramatic accentuation might also serve as a strategy of concealment—one of the strategies that a jockey must learn. Concealment strategies are particularly important in handicap races and trainers will caution riders *not to win by too much;* for an easy win will lead the track handicapper to add extra poundage on the horse in his next outing. If the jockey fails to conceal the true form of a handicap horse, the trainer will mete out sanctions, as Jockey Eddie Arcaro recalls:

> I won the Metropolitan with Third Degree by five lengths. That was a mile race. Handicapper John B. Campbell was so impressed by this performance that he tacked on more weight for Third Degree's Suburban Handicap engagement. That added weight proved to be the difference between victory and defeat. John Gaver [the trainer] gave me hell for that.[16]

16. Eddie Arcaro, *I Ride to Win* (New York: Greenberg, 1951), p. 39. The strategy of winning by the shortest possible margin is the key deceptive move of the pool room hustler. See Ned Polsky, "The Hustler," in *Hustlers, Beats, and Others* (Chicago: Aldine Publishing Company, 1967).

A DAY IN THE LIFE OF A JOCKEY

Unless the jockey exercises horses in the morning or is called upon to have a dry run with a horse in preparation for some big engagement, his working day begins at noon. At that time, he checks into the jockeys' quarters located near the paddock (where the horses will be saddled before each race). By the time the jock arrives, the valets will already have been at work for a few hours, polishing boots and saddles and checking the colors to be worn by the riders. The silks (the shirts that bear the colors of the owner) are brought in from the "color room" and hung on racks in the order of each race and each starting position. When the jock arrives, he heads straight for the steam room or the whirlpool bath, and then sits down in the locker room to leaf through the *Racing Form* or josh with the valets.

By 12:30, the patrol judge or one of the stewards announces he is going to screen films of the previous day's races. This is known as the jockeys' matinee. Attendance is optional, except for those jockeys who are specifically ordered to attend. From time to time, the judge will stop the film to point out incidents of misconduct, or—in the case of apprentice jocks—he may point out mistakes and offer advice.

Before each race, the jockey's weight is checked in the weighing room. He weighs in wearing his colors, carrying his equipment—and nothing else. If he has a cigarette in his mouth, he won't be weighed.

Afterwards, he goes to the paddock where the trainer and sometimes the owner will be waiting in a stall with the same number as the post position of the horse. The horse has already been saddled and either is standing in the stall or is being paraded around the paddock, led by the groom or hotwalker. Now the trainer instructs the jockey: "This horse has been primed for this race; keep him close to the pace and when the early runners fade go to the whip—and come home early."

Parading to the starting gate, the jock looks over at the tote board and sees his horse is 3 to 1. He feels a little more confident knowing that so many fans have thought highly of his chances. Also, with all that money riding on him, he knows he must look good. Now he's at the starting gate, and finally, in his stall. All the mounts are in. Some of the boys are chanting: "No chance yet, sir; no chance; no chance, sir." Suddenly all is quiet and the starter presses the button releasing the gate.

It is a close race, but the jock's mount lasts to win. Returning to the winner's circle, he salutes the placing judges with his whip; failing to do so results in a fine. In the winner's circle, he is photographed along with the trainer, the owner and his wife, and friends of the family. Returning to the jockeys' quarters, he can relax if he doesn't ride in the next race. In the jockeys' quarters, he sees some of the other jocks relaxing, watching television, playing cards, pool, or ping-pong. Others are in the heat box or in a bunk bed swathed in rubber sheets.

After his last mount of the day, the jock can leave the jockeys' quarters. He then goes to the club house or turf club where his agent has been playing the horses and talking to the trainers. He consults with the agent as to his future mounts. He stays to watch a race or two, very often as a guest in the private box of one of the owners or trainers. Once the jockey leaves the park, his racing day is over. But the working day is far from over for the trainers and the other men behind the horse.

4.

THE MAN BEHIND THE HORSE

CAPTAIN OF THE STABLE

The trainer is responsible for bringing a horse up to a race, for deciding (for the owner) when a horse is ready to bet, and for buying and selling animals. To his stable help—the grooms, exercise boys, hot walkers—he is the captain of a ship. His requests are commands. This command posture, in the typical case, even pervades interaction with the owner. Although paying a suitable amount of deference to his employer, the trainer jealously reserves the right to make all decisions. For instance, if the owner feels a horse should run on a particular day and the trainer insists otherwise, the owner more than likely will back down first. The trainer simply will tell the owner, "If you don't like the way I'm running things, take your stock elsewhere."

The trainer's willingness to stand up to the owner regarding the handling of a horse—even if it means losing his employer's entire stable—is not a question of personal courage, but part of a structural feature of horse racing. In horse racing, a game of musical chairs is played vis-a-vis owners and trainers: if a trainer's barn is emptied by an irate owner, the trainer knows that the word will be spread that he is available and that he soon will be negotiating with another owner. Moreover, in a test of loyalty, stable employees typically will side with the trainer, and if a

47

split with the owner occurs, they will walk out with him. Therefore, the trainer is aware that, in his negotiations with the owner,
the latter must take into account that the trainer, despite his sub-
ordinate status, is bargaining from a position of strength.

On the other hand, the owner can achieve a measure of control over the trainer by invoking the widely accepted *intention-to-
dissolve rule:* If the trainer wishes to dissolve his working agreement with the owner, he is expected to give ninety days' notice;
if the owner wishes to dissolve, he may give only ten minutes'
notice.

As insurance against the obvious job insecurity resulting from
this practice, trainers generally seek simultaneous working agree-
ments with many different owners. An extreme illustration is the
case of one highly successful West Coast trainer who had more
than thirty horses in his barn, each of which had *different* owners.
With this kind of a "cushion," the typical trainer—in his disputes
with an owner—will comply with those requests that fall within
the former's "zone of indifference";[1] those that don't, he refuses.

What the trainer presumably has to offer an owner is expertise
in conditioning animals to win races. Getting a horse physically
ready for a race is a routine affair, however, and the amount of
expertise necessary for the job can easily be exaggerated. So long
as the horse doesn't suffer an illness, he typically responds to a
well-codified schedule. When the horse is brought into training,
he is run at a gallop two miles a day for a couple of weeks in a
process known as "legging up." If the horse comes back from his
daily gallop without breathing too hard, he is ready for short
workouts that emphasize speed. He will be raced at three furlongs
about twice a week. If his time is between 36 and 38 seconds, he
is then stretched out to the distance he will be asked to race (six
furlongs to $1\frac{1}{8}$ of a mile covers 95 per cent of all racing events).
As the day of racing approaches, his trainer will sharpen him with
shorter blowouts (three- or four-furlong workouts). When a horse

1. On the concept of "zone of indifference," see Chester I. Barnard,
The Functions of the Executive (Cambridge, Mass.: Harvard University
Press, 1938), pp. 168–169.

is claimed, he is by definition a horse in training, and the new trainer will continue to build on the previous trainer's work by blowing the horse out occasionally. If a horse has been rested for two months or longer, he will be brought back into training following the routine described here.

The significant difference in the skills of trainers lies not so much in their ability to get horses in condition for races, but in their ability to place horses in races where their animals will have an advantage unperceived by others, especially other trainers. This means that *the crucial skill for success is the ability to control appearances and to break through the controls of others.* In short, the racing game is played in terms of strategies of concealment and detection.

TYPES OF TRAINERS

The major distinction between trainers is that of "honest johns" and "manipulators." The former are nonbetting trainers; the latter, betting trainers. The manipulators, in turn, fall into the "lone wolf" and the "syndicate" categories while the honest johns are further classified as the "headliner," the "horsetrader," and the "gyp." Again, I emphasize that these roles are simply conventional orientations adapted by certain social actors as a typical response to recurrent situations.

Manipulators

I shall turn first to the manipulators—the betting trainers—and discuss the modes of strategy of the lone wolf and the syndicate man.

The Lone Wolf. All manipulators attempt to conceal the true form of their horses so that when making a bid to win a race, they will have advantageous odds. The characteristic of the lone wolf is that he shares this information with no one, and when the time comes to bet, he uses his own money. For the lone wolf, as for other manipulators, betting constitutes a major or substantial part of his income. But the lone wolf's style gives him advantages not available to the other manipulators. Because his information is not shared, the mutuel payoffs on his horses are protected: no large heaps of "smart money" are placed on his chargers to depress the odds. Thus, while the syndicate man seldom gets more than 4 to 1 on his "ripe" horses, the lone wolf often gets 10 to 1 or more on his ready animals. Also the longer the odds, the less he needs to bet to make a substantial profit—an important consideration since he bets with his own money. In short, the good prices he receives depend on his being the tightest-lipped of a tight-lipped breed.

Since the lone wolf wishes to protect the price, that is, the odds, he does not bet through a bookie. Experience has shown him that bookies have ways of tampering with the odds: an "inside man" can put down a wad of cash at the track, depressing the odds on the lone wolf's sleeper. Aside from such tampering, the lone wolf knows he cannot get more than 20-to-1 odds from a bookie. That is, even if a horse pays $60 for each $2 bet, the bookie's payoff would be only $42. And frequently, bookies will simply refuse to accept the lone wolf's bets. Unlike prostitutes, bookies do not service clients on a universal basis, but rather cultivate a steady clientele of sure losers. Of course, the lone wolf could get others to put down bets for him with a bookie—but that means sharing knowledge. Thus, the lone wolf plays at the track.

Characteristically, then, the lone wolf plays at the track, invests his own money, and is the most extreme case of restricting information about his intentions. This does not mean, however, that he always works alone. Rather he sometimes employs a "beard," or front man.

In the days before parimutuel betting, the beard was an essential accomplice of the manipulator, permitting him to protect the odds. Bookies, operating at the track, would either refuse the bet of the manipulator, or offer him such low odds as to make all the manipulating a waste. The operations of Pittsburgh Phil, reputedly the greatest of all punters in horseracing lore, set the pattern for the use of the beard and turned betting on horses into a game of

upon to carry 126 pounds if he races that Saturday in a similar race. So the trainer will race the horse next time for a higher claiming tag, not with the intention of winning—for the horse is unlikely to run creditably in a higher class—but with the aim of keeping it in condition while time passes and a race can be found where the horse can carry less weight and still meet $3,500 competition.

When a trainer runs his $3,500 horse for a higher claiming tag, he generally will instruct the jockey not to press the horse. If the horse performs dismally at the higher tag, other trainers will conclude that the horse is not a worthwhile claim. (A bargain horse is considered to be one that can be bought at a lower price and then "stepped up" to win at a higher price. A trainer who makes these kinds of claims is known as a "halterman"—and a good halterman is the envy of the racing fraternity; he is the trainer's trainer.)

Now, since the horse has been running without being pressed at the higher claiming price, it will need at least one race in its own company to get back in sharp form. Thus, the trainer may drop the horse down to its proper company of $3,500, but race the horse into condition—that is, give the jockey instructions to rush the horse in front and then ease up or to run it very late. In either case, the horse will get "legged up" but not expend too much energy—and perhaps get a piece of the purse. In the next outing, the trainer will have his legged-up animal primed for an all-out effort. About a month has passed since the horse's last winning effort, and now it can race in its proper company at a weight it can carry. (Horsemen believe that high weight and strenuous effort cripples horses.) By this time, the public has grown somewhat cool on the horse, and it will not go to the post as a favorite. The honest john cares nothing about that; his routine strategy is to save his horse from the claiming box and maintain its soundness. The syndicate man, on the other hand, uses the same strategy —but to get favorable odds.

The lone wolf employs a wider repertoire of concealment strategies; for his purpose is to keep his horse under wraps until "box-car mutuels" are expected. His $3,500 horse will win, and then lose ten races in a row in very poor performances before it suddenly wins again for $3,500. Such horses are called erratic in-and-outers, thought to be physically unsound. In this manner, the lone wolf is protected against having his betting tool claimed away. Evidence that an in-and-outer quality is characteristic of the horseman and not the horse shows up when such a horse is claimed: suddenly, in a new barn, it runs with consistency.

To get a horse to lose, the lone wolf (and, to a much lesser extent, the syndicate man) will use one or more of a wide range of tactics: If his horse is a sprint horse, he will run it in distance races, where its ability will be unperceived; if his horse is a distance horse, the reverse strategy will be employed. If the horse runs well only when on the pace, the jockey will be instructed to come from behind; if the horse can only give one good run from behind, the jockey will be told to force the pace. If the horse runs well with blinkers or a certain type of shoe, the trainer—on losing efforts—will run the horse without blinkers or with inappropriate shoes. If his horse will extend himself only on a fast (dry) track, he will enter the animal on muddy tracks. With each losing effort, the odds on the horse rise. On the day when the trainer shoots, all the conditions will be favorable for victory—shoes, track condition, equipment, distance of race, and so forth.

Racing officials are well aware of this chicanery, and trainers who continually employ these tactics are investigated by a secret service (known as the Thoroughbred Racing Protective Bureau) of the racing association to see if they have gambling connections. Paradoxically, the syndicate man—who does have gambling connections—is not investigated; for the performance of his horses indicates he is running a clean stable. Racing officials have arbitrary power, and as a working (though unstated) rule-of-thumb, they tolerate an "honest" stable (one that limits the use of concealment devices) operated by the syndicate man and a "dishonest" stable (one that makes much use of concealment devices) operated by a lone wolf with no gambling connections. The lone wolf and the syndicate man can continue their operations with relative impunity; only the combination of devious manipulation and known gambling connections makes a trainer *persona non grata.* In their own way, then, the syndicate man and the lone wolf are conforming to official expectations, and in this manner they establish what might be called the "deviance credits" [5] that permit them to escape from official punishment—despite the element of shadiness characterized by both types of operation.

In my remarks so far, I have indicated that the lone wolf surprises with sudden "wakeups," while the syndicate man runs horses with relatively exposed form. An exception to this rule is the 2-year-old race. The value of inside information is seen most clearly in such races; here the syndicate man really earns his fee. Knowledge of a 2-year-old's true form is traditionally the exclusive property of the stable until it is exposed by winning. Until a stable is ready for the "crackdown," a 2-year-old can run as "stiff" as the trainer desires without incurring the critical comments of either the officials or the public. Overtly, all persons connected with racing subscribe to the theory that baby horses discover their legs all at once. So when a 2-year-old romps home easily paying $100, no one makes accusations of a fixed race. Covertly, a stable may legitimately plan a coup under this unstated rule: the coup must involve a 2-year-old that has never won. Perhaps one reason for the permissive attitude toward the 2-year-old coup is that, since the horse has never won a race, the element of risk still looms large and the "sure-thing race" remains problematic.

The only way the form of a 2-year-old can be discerned is by the time of its workouts. When the manipulating trainer works his horse in secret for speed, he is said be "working a horse by lantern." The horse is worked just at daybreak before the clockers arrive to observe the scene. To further conceal its form, the rider working the horse is, whenever possible, an apprentice who is bound legally and morally to secrecy.

Once the syndicate man has tipped his hot 2-year-old, the betting ring (or clients) are themselves responsible to avoid disclosing the information to the public. If the betting ring places its bets away from the track, it will split up the bets among a number

5. The concept of "deviance credits" is taken from E. P. Hollander, "Conformity, Status, and Idiosyncrasy Credit," *Psychological Review*, 65 (1958), especially p. 120.

of agents throughout the country so as not to attract attention or get "comeback money." (When a horse gets "hot," as bookies term it, they lay off bets. If time permits, money goes back to the track and is called comeback money.) When this strategy is not feasible, some money will be placed with one or two bookies and some at the track, or at the track only.

The odds on a horse are depressed in two ways. The first is the *primary wager* (that is, the money bet by the gamblers themselves). Naturally, the more one bets on an animal, the lower its odds. Gamblers regard this phenomenon as a fact of nature, as the immutable law of self-destroying information. (The very process of using reliable information lessens its value; therefore it limits the amount one wagers.) But the much more significant way in which odds are depressed is the *secondary play*.

To illustrate secondary play, consider the following: Suppose a horse that is 10 to 1 on the morning line suddenly drops to 3 to 1 about five minutes after the betting windows open. The public takes this as a sign of a hot thing: smart money is being played, so it thinks. Then the bandwagon effect begins, and despite the absence of "cold form" (information concerning the good form of a horse derived wholly from the racing charts), the horse will be heavily bet and leave the starting gate perhaps at even money. The odds on the horse have been depressed because of secondary play.

If such a horse wins, players have the satisfaction of having detected the smart-money action. Actually, these horses win enough times to keep players alert to the smart money. However, contrary to most players' beliefs, this smart money is not stable money or the money of smart gamblers operating with inside information. Rather, it is bookie comeback money placed during the early betting in one lump sum in order to depress the odds and engineer a bandwagon effect. Bookies do this most often in 2-year-old races, when a stable may have a world-beater under wraps. If a big bet on it comes in, the bookies will send it back to the track, engineer a bandwagon, and the 20-to-1 longshot that has never won a race goes off at even money. I might point out that the bookie bets just enough to start the bandwagon, then arranges to make a profit if the horse loses or to break even if the horse wins. In this illustration, the secondary play has been engineered. Sometimes, the bandwagon can be triggered by an untutored player who has received reliable information and overanxiously has tried to capitalize on it, placing huge bets shortly after the sellers' windows open.

To avoid the bandwagon effect, the trainer's client will restrain himself from overloading the bookie; and at the track he will place his bets as close to post-time as possible. The tote changes odds every ninety seconds, the last change occurring after the horses have left the gate. One can observe occasionally that during the running of the race a horse will drop from, say, 5 to 1 to 3 to 1, this being the action of smart money, too late to be detected by the public. The trainer's client will walk up to the $50 or $100 window at one minute before post-time and have the seller keep punching tickets until the machines are locked (by the starter, some ten seconds after the horses have left the gate). The later the betting action, the less likely will others be able to capitalize on the information communicated by a drop in odds.

Honest Johns

The distinguishing mark of the honest johns is their lack of interest in turning a profit by betting. There are three types of honest johns: "headliners," "horsetraders," and "gyps." Although honest johns are not concerned with manipulating a horse for a bet, they do manipulate the showings of their horses, and the tactics that they employ vary for different types of horses.

Headliners. Headliners are men who train for stables owned by elite society—the Vanderbilts, the Whitneys, the Woodwards, and so forth—who breed their own horses and whose sole concern is with winning the most coveted races. No claiming horses reside in these barns. If a horse can't win nonclaiming races, it is sold at public auction or private transaction. The trainers employed by these owners do not own any horses of their own, nor do they operate a public stable (that is, take on horses for more than one owner). In addition to the regular 10 per cent received for each winning race, these trainers also command a basic salary, averaging better than $10,000 a year.

While the manipulator attempts to conceal the form of his chargers to get a big price, the headliner conceals the form of his horses to get low weight. The natural enemy of the headliner is the track handicapper. As previously mentioned, the track handicapper assigns the weight to the various horses in such a manner that theoretically they will all reach the finish line together. The problem of the trainer then is to win without his horse looking too good. In a big race, the trainer will never tell the jockey to "get out and win the race and don't look back." If a horse wins a handicap race easily, it will be severely penalized in future weight assignments. Thus the strategy is to win with a horse by a *short* margin. Since it is difficult to control the winning distance of a front-running animal, headliners prefer to train their horses to run from off the pace, and sometimes from far off the pace. Of course, the price one pays for training a horse to run that way is the risk that a front-running horse will steal the race. To counter this, the trainer often employs a strategy known as "whipsawing." Here, the trainer will run an "entry" of two or more horses. The "big horse" will rest comfortably in the rear of the pack while the other horse in the entry will run to the front, wiping out the front-running competition. If the strategy is successful, the front-running animals will exhaust each other, and the star will move up as late as possible overhauling the opposition in the last few yards. Winning so closely, it will not be penalized more than a pound or two in the next handicap it is entered. In the days before the advent of the film patrol, the practice of whipsawing was more effective than today; competitors were thrown off stride by fouling, bumping, and other illegal but hard-to-detect acts. In addition, if one part of an entry engaged in a foul, it did not reflect on the other part of the entry. Today the racing rules hold that if a stable enters two or more horses in a race and if one horse is disqualified for any reason, then the other part of the entry is also disqualified, even if it was not a participant in the foul.

Whipsawing remains an effective strategy and the best defense is counterwhipsawing. That is, the opposition will also run an entry, perhaps with three horses: one horse will be used to wipe out the front-running opposition, and then the second horse will be sent for the lead, forcing the big horse of the opposition to make an early move; meanwhile, the big horse of the counter-whipsawing stable can remain in the rear until ready to make his move.

Racing fans enjoy speculating before a big handicap event on just what strategy will be employed. Most are well aware that trainers attempt to whipsaw with an entry. But what many fans find incredible is that when there is no entry (two or more horses in a race from the same stable), horsemen—by an unstated common understanding—cooperate to bring about the same results. The phenomenon deserves a special name, which might serve as a sensitizing concept for further investigation. I will refer to it as the "deference boon."

By the deference boon, I mean the unstated, largely unconscious, cooperation of individuals to permit a rival of higher social status to succeed in a competitive game.

A richly documented example of the deference boon deserves brief summary here—the study of the bowling activities of the Norton Gang as described by William F. Whyte.[6] Whyte noted that the bowling scores of the Nortons depended on whether they bowled individually or in team competition. Individually, lower-ranking members of the gang demonstrated substantial ability, but in full-scale competition with other gang members, the scores of the players followed almost exactly the status of the gang members. One could predict the outcome of a competitive event, not by an analysis of the ability of the players, but by their status in the gang. Moreover, Whyte notes that gang members unconsciously cooperated to "permit" the higher status members to win.

The deference boon is one of the observable features of allowance races (nonclaiming races that carry a purse slightly greater than claiming races). If in such a race only one horse is entered from an elite stable and if the horse is a favorite who has dis-

6. William F. Whyte, *Street Corner Society* (Chicago: University of Chicago Press, 1943), especially chapter 2, "Bowling and Social Ranking."

played recent form, a common understanding exists among the other trainers and jockeys that this horse *should* win (in other words, it is morally right).[7] Observing several hundred such races over the years, I have noted that these horses win without being pressed too hard and in slower time than recent previous performances. The instructions of "deferring" trainers is something like: "If you think you have a chance to win it, go ahead; but don't press the horse for second money." To the jockey such instructions mean: "This is not a race to try to win." Consider, then, a typical situation: the jockey on Poor George will understand the trainer's message that today is not a winning day. Meanwhile, Elite Horse, from the elite stable, is the favorite; and Slow Poke, a front runner, is the contender. When the race begins, Slow Poke goes to the front. But unexpectedly Poor George is right there running with him and "burning him out." The horses race head and head until the stretch and then Elite Horse casually bypasses them to win an easy victory.

To the player, such a race often looks like a "boat race" (a fixed or prearranged race). What allays suspicion is that the winning horse is a favorite (and why bother to fix a favorite?), and second, the winning stable has elite connections (such people don't put in a fix). Yet the race has been "fixed" by a common understanding—the result of the deference boon.

Evidence to support these observations on the deference boon is hard to come by. But its operation is indicated in remarks made by trainers taking their places in the stands to watch the race. To be sure, not every trainer is approachable, especially by strangers. But when I have succeeded in getting a trainer to talk about how his animal would fare in an allowance race, he might remark that his horse had a chance but often add that another horse was "ex-

7. David Matza has suggested to me that two sets of considerations may be operative in the "deference boon." The first is the hierarchical arrangement external to the activity in question, for example, the status of the Nortons in the gang. The second is the hierarchical arrangement internal to the activity, for example, the status of the Nortons vis-à-vis the ordering of bowling skills. Matza's internal-external distinction appears relevant to bowling, poker, and other activities where the same participants are involved in the activity in question. Matza's comment is clearly deserving of further research.

pected to win." Only when the favorite was from an elite barn was I told by a trainer that another horse was "expected to win."

While elite stables will frequently win allowance races under the circumstances just described, they often hopelessly lose such races, even when their horses are odds-on favorites. In such races, the headliner merely intends to give the horse a prep for a big race and not to win. (Usually the jockey is told that under no circumstances is he to use a whip.) Other trainers are well aware that a rich feature race is, let us say, a week or so off, and the star has been entered in a current race as a prep for the future engagement. Because of the entrance of a big-name horse in the allowance race, the players regard the animal as the class-of-the-field and back him heavily. Thus, other trainers with horses too good for claiming races and not good enough for handicap and stakes races will be sending out animals in a race that they can win—and get a good price (since an odds-on favorite in the field boosts the odds of all the other horses considerably). For these trainers, such a race is a gravy race, regarded as a *noblesse oblige* offering. In no other type of race can a trainer command such big odds on a horse with exposed form. But when the elite stable has a horse of only allowance caliber and is in form and thus meant to win, we find the reciprocal debt paid off.

Racing officials look on the practice of prepping a big horse in an allowance race as an acceptable, though not preferred, routine; and the headliner who loses in such a race is not subjected to the inquisition reserved for others under similar circumstances. Here, then, is one setting where the officials do not protect the public. Officials are hesitant to press trainers of elite stables, whose owners are often on the board of governors and in other ways may serve as officials. Thus a type of double standard of justice is practiced at the track. In other words, differential sanctioning is a function of the deviant's status.

Before closing this section, I wish to point up one major exception to what I have said about concealment strategies. I refer to 2-year-old stakes races, virtually the only races where candidness is the rule, not the exception. Here concealment of maximum abilities is unnecessary; in fact, in this kind of race the trainer will instruct the jockey to push the horse, if possible, to a decisive victory. If anything, the strategy is to make the animal appear even better than it is. The reason for this is not hard to understand: in 2-year-old stakes all the entrants carry the same weight, regardless of past performance. Another reason for making a horse look even better than his real ability is to discourage competition. Owners of 2-year-olds must pay periodic fees for stakes races whether their horses run or not; so they are tempted to race their animals if they feel they have any kind of chance. Consequently, 2-year-old races tend to be overcrowded, and very often the best horse loses because it gets caught in a traffic jam. The problem of the overcrowded field is further accentuated since races for younger animals are typically sprints—the shorter the race, the greater the problem of a crowded field. Thus, nonclaiming 2-year-olds are run honestly (that is, pressed to their utmost to win by the largest possible margin)—first, because no weight penalty is attached after an easy win; second, because owners wish to discourage competition in order to keep the fields from becoming rough-and-tumble cavalry charges.

The Horsetrader. We have seen that the headliner, even as a species of the genre honest johns, uses concealment and subterfuge. While this is also true of the horsetrader, he must in addition specialize in detecting the deception of the other trainers. Specifically, he is concerned with finding horses of a higher class whose true abilities are being concealed and are running at a lower-class level. He is out to detect such horses, claim them, step them up in class, and win. If he is successful, he is known as a good halterman. Combined with this quality, he is also characterized by having many claims and a good deal of turnover of horses in his stable, and thus he is called a "horsetrader."

The horsetrader generally does not own his own horses, but trains for a large public stable. Most of his chargers are platers, with a sprinkling of allowance horses, and perhaps one handicap or stakes runner. His owners are middle-class businessmen who seldom engage in the risky and expensive enterprise of breeding their own stock or purchasing yearlings to be developed. They break into the game by buying a horse-in-training at a private sale and then applying for an owner's license. The purchased horse is known as a "policeman," an ineffectual animal that nevertheless serves a useful purpose. Once the policeman is run in a race at the track, the owner is qualified to claim a horse. Having claimed an animal, the owner is really in business with a running horse, and the policeman is quickly discarded.

One reason the policeman is quickly discarded (often for less than its purchase price) is because the horsetrader does not tolerate ineffectual animals. He wants only winning horses in his barn and searches continually for spots where they can win. The horsetrader takes pride not only in his honesty (that is, he doesn't bet but shoots only for purses), but in his ability to judge and evaluate horseflesh and his ability to condition animals. When he tells the owner that his horse is "fresh and fit and ready to win," he stands behind the assertion and is willing to put his reputation on the line. Should the horse lose under these circumstances he must be ready, as we will shortly see, with a mitigating excuse.

Understandably, the betting owner with shady connections prefers the honest john trainer because his reputation is such that track officials are not likely to watch him and his associates closely. In addition, the betting owner gravitates toward those trainers (invariably horsetraders) who have the reputed ability to state with certainty the condition of an animal and the probable outcome of a race. When the trainer tells the owner that the horse is fit and ready, the owner acts decisively—betting confidently and accepting gladly any price he can get. Here, then, is an instance of an owner, not a trainer, who is wired to betting connections that may lay bets with the books throughout the country.

The Gyp. A man honest by default, the gyp is the trainer who keeps body and soul together by managing an occasional winner and by getting pieces of purses. Even fourth money of $75 or $150 helps pay the carrot man, the blacksmith, or the veterinarian. He owns the horses he trains, and because of this has a certain pride of ownership that he feels the more successful horsetrader lacks. He is known as a gyp (short for gypsy) partly because he moves about more than other trainers, shifting from track to track where he can find races cheap enough for his cheap platers.

But he is also a gypsy in his mode of life—his rather ragged appearance, his home in the hay, his diet of carrots (which he shares with the horses) and fried potatoes (when money becomes too short for even the inexpensive track kitchen).

The gyp, then, is the *lumpenproletariat* of the trainers' status world. To the lone wolf trainer, the gyp is a portrait of a man who plays the game for purses; to the syndicate trainer, a man who has lost his connections; to the headliners and the horse-traders, a man who is plagued by bad luck. To all, he is a nuisance who is taking up good stable space with plugs. And yet to all, he is a kind of mascot.

As a mascot, he is often subjected to good-natured ridicule. For instance, the gyp's horses are typically "cripples" with puffed ankles, bowed tendons, and bucked shins, and when he is seen walking his animals about the barn area, the stage is set for one of the recurrent whimsical scenes involving the gyp:

Horsetrader (to Gyp walking his "cripple"): Hey, Red! What are you going to do with that horse?

Gyp: Why, race him, of course.

Horsetrader: By gosh, I think you can beat him.

As a butt of such ribbing, the gyp is often cooperative, like the straight man in a comedy routine. Sometimes he has the punch line, as when the gyp makes mock challenges to headliners for a match race between a handicap star and his cripple.

Among a group of men whose trademark is secrecy, social distance, austerity, and deception, the gyp's ingenuousness, free-and-easy ways, and open-faced bluntness is refreshing. In terms of the trainer's normative patterns of behavior, the gyp is a deviant. But he is the kind of in-group deviant [8] who is protected by informal understanding and formal ruling. For instance, some gyps have only one horse (or only one horse during a given meet) that is in

8. For a useful discussion of the in-group deviant see Robert A. Dentler and Kai T. Erikson, "The Functions of Deviance in Groups," *Social Problems,* 7 (1959), pp. 98–107.

racing condition. An unwritten rule in horse racing is that one doesn't claim a man's last horse. Thus the gyp can run a $2,500-class animal in $2,000 claiming races week after week with confidence that it won't be claimed, each time picking up a piece of the purse. The point is that, by common understanding, the gyps are permitted to get their share.

Under unusual conditions, an owner will pressure his trainer to put in a claim for a gyp's only horse. When the trainer does consent to do so, he invariably adds the condition that the owner personally notify the gyp just before putting in the claim—on the assumption that once the owner talks to the man, he will back out; and in fact, this is what frequently happens. Few owners can carry through with their plans in the face of an emotional display where the gyp pours out his tears or rage when he finds some owner intends to claim his only animal. Moreover, the owner's actions are not sanctioned by the racing fraternity; so he usually hesitates to make such a claim.

Because some owners enter the racing world with a business-is-business ethic, a formal rule serves to cushion the plight of the one-horse trainer and keep him in business. According to the ruling, if a man has his only horse claimed, he is permitted sixty days to make a "free claim." Since most meets are less than fifty days, that means that a gyp who loses his horse at one circuit can claim a horse at another circuit, even though he has not raced a horse on the new circuit. For example, if the gyp has his only horse claimed at Golden Gate Race Track in northern California, he might—without racing a horse—be free to claim an animal a month or more later at Hollywood Park in southern California. This is a potent option; for it is in the early days of racing at a new meet, and especially on the first day of racing that horses run in claiming races below their usual class level. Trainers are more willing to enter horses below their usual class on opening day because no owner—with the exception of those possessing a free claim—can claim a horse if he has not run one on the grounds of a new meet. To illustrate, in the first race of opening day at Hollywood Park, if there are seven horses entered, then only those seven owners can make a claim in that race—plus the man with a free claim. Of course, in making a claim, the gyp must put down in cash the full claiming price; in this sense, there is nothing free about a free claim.

THE USES OF EXCUSES

Consider the following encounter:

A trainer is approached by an owner, who says that his fried chicken home-delivery service is not doing too well but that he would like to pick up another horse or two—which he could swing if he could cash a few good bets. The owner asks the trainer for a tip on one of his likeliest chargers (which may be a horse owned by someone else in the trainer's public stable).

With the betting spot found, the trainer will prompt the owner to unbuckle his money belt. The owner, in turn, may be wired to betting connections (that is, in league with a professional gambling crowd, which salts the owner's kitty in exchange for hot information).

In the paddock, the trainer reveals to the jockey that the horse has been primed for the upcoming race, and further encourages the boy with the promise of a little something extra for bringing his mount home first. A little something extra means either 15 per cent of the purse (instead of the usual 10 per cent) or a $50 win ticket on the horse. The owner, not the trainer, pays for these extras.

Many of these planned killings fizzle out because the horse is not ready; the trainer has miscalculated the condition of his animal. Now one of the most important self-professed characteristics of the trainer is that he is the only one who *really* knows the current condition of his horse. For a trainer to say that he is unsure of his horse's fitness is comparable to a doctor's saying that he doesn't know if his patient is ill or well. In fact, both doctors and trainers are often guessing; but unlike doctors, the trainer cannot check his guesses by asking his animal how he feels. Nevertheless, if a trainer announces that his horse is in condition for a winning race and the horse runs poorly, he is held responsible. Indeed, his very reputation as a trainer is discredited.

When a trainer instructs a jockey in the paddock to press the horse "all out" for a winning effort and the horse fails to respond well, the jockey knows—barring the factor of racing luck (for example, the horse being blocked or put in a pocket, etc.)—that his mount was not raced to the peak condition the trainer had assumed. If the "well-meant" horse thus fails to run close up because it was not legged up sufficiently, the jockey is in a position to embarrass the trainer.

For a jockey to tell a trainer that a horse that showed poorly was not in condition would be an open affront to the trainer's identity as one with superior knowledge of horseflesh. What the trainer expects to hear from the jockey is a "reasonable account" for the horse's loss. (When the trainer's reputation is at stake, blaming inadequate conditioning is not considered "reasonable." However, if the owner is not backing the horse and if the trainer informs the jockey that the condition of the animal is uncertain, the boy will give an honest evaluation and say, "The horse was short," or "He wouldn't extend himself," or "He should be ready next time.")

Let me emphasize that when the trainer asks the jockey why his horse lost what was to be a winning race, the trainer *doesn't want the truth, he wants reasonableness.*[9] If the jockey wishes to ride for this trainer again, he will fashion an appropriate excuse: that he was bumped on the turn, that the horse stumbled at the start, or was caught flatfooted when the gate opened, and so forth. These accounts are reasonable; for in every race most horses have *some* mishap. The jockey is not entirely lying, merely exaggerating the difficulty to give an account that will help the trainer save face.

Now according to the unwritten contract between the trainer and the owner, when the former tells the latter that a horse will

9. David Sudnow has similarly found that the public defender, when interrogating his client, is concerned not with truth but "reasonableness." See Sudnow's "Normal Crimes," *Social Problems,* 12 (Winter 1965), pp. 255–276.

win and advises him to make heavy bets, *the trainer must deliver.* And this unwritten law is invoked by the owner whenever the trainer fails—unless of course his responsibility is voided by a reasonable account.[10] The trainer, in short, must have a rich and ready repertoire of excuses.[11] Another recurrent scene at the track is the trainer explaining to the owner what went wrong, often passing on the jockey's account: "Tough break. The boy had to steady the horse when it got tight in the stretch."

The betting public's image of the trainer is that of a crook who will "stiff" a horse (hold his horse back) whenever he feels the odds on his animal are too low to warrant a good bet. This image is part of racing folklore, having only a modicum of truth to it. Still, racing officials feel obliged to investigate the possibility of a horse being pulled and to preserve the good will of the patrons they will often conduct an investigation whenever a hot favorite ran poorly though not suffering any apparent mishap.

In most races, the trainer has little expectation of winning. When a horse has not indicated good recent form, the trainer and the betting public view the horse's losing effort as a normal event. On other occasions, the horse may have shown good recent form, but the trainer has no intention of winning (for example, he may enter a horse to let it unwind after a previous tough race or to breeze the animal before it is sent to the farm for a rest or shipped to another track). When such a horse is heavily bet but runs poorly, the betting public usually suspects chicanery (of course, some trainers occasionally will stiff a horse simply to jack up the price on future outings), and it demands through the intermediary of the racing officials a reason for the discrepant occurrence— the trainer is accountable.

In this case, the trainer may give an account that would be unreasonable in an owner's eyes but perfectly reasonable to a board of inquiry. For instance, the trainer may say—to the offi-

10. For a general statement that has direct relevance to the present discussion see H. L. A. Hart, "Ascription of Responsibility," in A. Flew (Ed.), *Language and Logic, Series I* (Oxford: Basil Blackwell).

11. If these excuses are not available, the trainer can resort finally to a promise that next time the horse will really be sharp and a planned coup will unquestionably succeed.

cials but not to the owner—that the horse was "off his oats," not in his best condition and that it refused to extend itself.

An ironclad excuse may be obtained from a *validating agent*, frequently a veterinarian. A vet might find any one of a number of infirmities in examining a horse that ran poorly: blood in its nostrils, speedy cuts, bruises, and so on. Passing on these findings to an inquiry board, the trainer is taken off the hook. (However, if the trainer is frequently called down for the inconsistency of his horses' performances, he might be denied stable space. This is one of the track's most effective sanctions against the deviant trainer.)

Reasonable accounts are of two orders—*legitimate* and *illegitimate*. To say that the horse bled in the race—this being validated by a veterinarian—would constitute a legitimate account for the horse's poor performance. An illegitimate account, though still reasonable, would be that the horse had some blood in his nostrils a few days before the race, but the trainer had not taken it seriously. Here, the trainer would be admonished for entering the horse in the first place. Still he is, in a sense, off the hook. But to say, "I pulled the horse to get better odds" would be considered *unreasonable* and would result in the officials ruling the trainer off the track, or they might simply regard him as insane.

As the above discussion suggests, excuses are a fundamental device used to restore stability in ruptured social relations. Further research on excuses should specify their ability to shore up the timbers of fractured sociation, their ability to throw bridges between the promised and the performed, their ability to repair the broken and restore the estranged.

SUPPORTING ROLES

The stable area is the track's backstage, and the people who work there are called "backstretch" personnel because they view the afternoon races in an area of the oval known as the backstretch—the area farthest from the paying spectators. Life in the backstage area has something of the character of a "total institution"—that is, an area where people work, sleep, and recreate.[12] As Devereux notes, the race track provides scope for entire careers, and few persons in it ever leave. "The specialized skills developed at the race track are not adaptable to other industries. Moreover, the people who work at the track are isolated from normal channels of interaction with the broader community as a result of physical, spatial, psychological, and social barriers." [13]

From the observer's point of view, the backstretch people—mostly grooms, who care for the horses—are locked in a community from which there is little escape. However, from the actors' point of view, they wouldn't, they say, trade their job for comparable ones on the "outside."

Grooms

For every three horses stabled at the track, there is one groom (or "guinea" as he is frequently called), who typically sleeps in the barn area attached to the horses' stalls. Married grooms often live in trailers near the track. Since the working day begins at 4:30 A.M., they engage in few if any outside activities even if they live off the track. Although the status of the groom on a societal level is probably very low, he has little outside interaction to confirm this negative image.

Perhaps because of the highly monotonous day of the groom —a routine that is unchanging and based wholly on the universal training schedule geared to the requirements of the horses—time for him has a static quality. The future is highly predictable: a recurrent cycle of movement from track to track—the same track during the same season of every year. Time is measured not by the calendar but by the racing season. The past is punctuated by the emergence of a great horse, and the benchmarks of the passing of time are referred to as "the year of Whirlaway," "the year of Citation," and so forth. For the backstage people, everyone has the same big clock.

12. For an explication of the concept of total institution see Goffman, *Asylums, op. cit.*
13. Devereux, *op. cit.,* p. 252.

Grooms are recruited largely from the ranks of trainers who have failed to make the grade or of exercise boys who have become too crippled, old, or heavy to ride. Many are simply relatives of owners, trainers, jockeys, agents, and other horsemen. One gets the job through "pull," and the major qualification is to "be good around animals." So if the groom can stay sober, it is easy enough for him to get and hold a job. His major duties are to rub down the horses, apply medication, walk, water, and feed them, and in general serve as a nursemaid.

There are compensations for the grooms: the traditionally excellent track kitchens (where one can "pitch until you win," that is, eat until he is stuffed), the many golf and baseball tournaments held in the track's infield, and a strong mutual bond of common fate. Because of this in-group solidarity, the possibility exists that a trainer's intentions may be circulated. Since all trainers have an interest in concealing information, they are secretive about their intentions and, if any information is given to the groom, it is often deliberate misinformation. Certainly, plans of a betting coup would never be divulged to a groom.

Owners

In discussing jockeys and trainers, I have made frequent reference to owners, treating them as a generic category. But it would be false to assume that owners are cast from the same mold.

To the trainer the owner is often little more than a necessary evil, an outsider who doesn't know the boundaries of his legitimate rights. While *competition* is the characteristic of trainer-trainer relations, *conflict* often characterizes trainer-owner relations. The major source of conflict involves rights of control versus rights of ownership. As mentioned earlier, the trainer jealously reserves the right to make all decisions, and to him the privilege of ownership means only the right to demand profit. Even here, the only profit the owner should demand is that from purses. For instance, if a trainer develops a young horse and someone offers a fat price for the animal, the owner—the trainer believes—has no right to sell the horse. The owner, however, has

entered into the world of horse racing bringing with him a different concept of property norms. These differences are seldom ironed
out in open discussion. Rather, the trainer accepts the owner's
definition (of property norms) as a fact of life and overcomes it
by strategy. Thus, the trainer who has developed an unraced animal will conceal its quality (from the owner) until it makes it
evident by winning several races. How to conceal information
from owners is one of the main topics of discussion among fellow
trainers and a fundamental source of their solidarity.

The techniques of dealing with hard-to-handle owners, then,
are learned from fellow colleagues. Dramaturgically considered, a
colleague is a person who gives the same type of performance, but
to a different audience.[14] Trainers swap stories about successful
encounters with owners, indicating what strategies serve to put
down overbearing owners.

It costs the owner about $5,000 a year to keep a horse. This
money is paid in monthly sums to the trainer, who in turn pays
the stable personnel. The trainer typically is not a salaried employee. The money he makes depends, ostensibly, on a 10 per cent
take of the winning purse. The purse distribution is split among
the first four horses: 65 per cent to the winner; 20 per cent to
second; 10 per cent to third; 5 per cent to fourth. At larger tracks,
the minimum purse is $3,000, or a split of $1,950, $600, $300, and
$150. Thus, the owner whose horse has in any year a record of
two wins and a second has had a free ride plus all the glory that
goes with ownership, while the trainer has earned $450.

The trainer looks at the economics of the relationship this way:
$450 a year is a small enough salary to demand the right of con-
trol, which is the right of total decision-making.

The size of an owner's stable influences his relations with the
trainer. The bigger the stable, the more likely the owner will exercise decision-making privileges. A large stable, owning more than
ten horses, often requires an office force, consisting of clerks,
bookkeepers, and accountants; and a field force, consisting of
exercise boys, farm managers, grooms, and so forth. (Some large
stables pay yearly salaries of more than $100,000.) In the case of

14. Goffman, *Presentation of Self, op. cit.,* p. 160ff.

a middle-sized stable, consisting of six to ten horses, its owner frequently can lure a trainer to drop other commitments and devote his sole attention to one stable. As suggested, the fewer the employers, the greater the control of any one employer. The owner can further assure a voice in decision-making by arranging a 50-50 split on profits with the trainer. Small stables, with two to four horses, invariably are turned over to a trainer who operates a public stable. The owners of small stables are the least likely to exercise decision-making privileges.

But more common than size is the classification that suggests the motivations of owners. In these terms, trainers type owners as "shopkeepers," "speed boys," or "sportsmen."

Shopkeepers. The shopkeeper is an entrepreneur who usually operates a self-sustaining enterprise—laundromats, cleaning establishments, restaurants—and has found in horse racing the risk-taking excitement that perhaps characterized his early days in business. He is willing and able to write off his losses; he is very satisfied if he can break even on his venture. Horse racing provides him (or his wife) with a daily leisure activity that confers upon him and his family the type of prestige that validates the status he has achieved in the business world.

This prestige is sufficient to keep the shopkeeper uncomplainingly paying the bills. But many shopkeepers are seeking something more. Before entering the game, they have typically been long-time occasional players. And like most players, they have come to believe that only those on the inside—the ones in the know—can really beat the game. A shopkeeper wants a peek at the backstage world where he can get access to information that will permit him to place winning bets. Thus, he demands from his trainer that he be reliably informed when one of his horses is ready to win. Aside from this, he follows the policy of noninterference with the activities and decisions of the trainer. This latter quality makes the shopkeeper popular with trainers. Something like 80 per cent of the owners are shopkeepers.

Speed Boys. A small percentage of owners turn to horse racing as a major financial enterprise whose success depends wholly on betting. Such an owner (called a speed boy) is usually a beard for a gambler who would be prohibited from acquiring an owner's license because of his background.

To ensure a trainer's compliance and secrecy, speed boys attempt to attract the services of a one-stable trainer; they invest in at least a middle-sized stable and often give the trainer 50 per cent of the purses. The trainer so employed must be willing to take orders: when to scratch a horse, where to place a horse, what horses to buy, and even how the horse is to be trained. The horses that are purchased, according to the directives of the speed boys, should have the capacity to run a winning race "wire to wire" (that is, from start to finish). As a betting tool, the front-running horse is unsurpassed. Because of his capacity to immediately take the lead, he not only saves the most ground (running close to the rail) but in addition avoids those difficulties (for example, getting blocked, bumped, placed in a pocket, etc.) that cause a horse to lose and are ordinarily written off as racing luck. In this manner, racing luck is overcome by advanced planning. When a front-running horse is owned by a speed boy, ridden by a "front-running jockey," and raced in his own class, it is the closest thing to a sure-bet race.

Sportsmen. Some owners are known as "lords of the turf"; their place in horse racing has been established by tradition. Others, with comparable racing establishments, represent new wealth. In either case, old wealth or new, they comprise the elite corps of racing owners—the sportsmen. (The distinction between old and new wealth to be found in certain locales in the parent society are maintained in the racing world. Thus sportsmen from old racing families are "lords of the turf," whereas new-wealth owners are often called "playboys." These differences, though invidious, are reflected in the public press. The *Racing Form*, for example, will refer to one owner as "one of the lords of the turf," and to another as "playboy owner Jones.")

From one point of view, the sportsman is the most desirable type of owner that a trainer can work for. The trainer shares the owner's prestige to some extent, he is assured high-quality horses, and typically he finds himself enjoying the security of a salaried position. These advantages are not wholly without a price—the trainer's renunciation of the right of control. Because many of the sportsmen are themselves horsemen (literally, in some cases, as indicated in their skill at the gentleman's game of polo), and because many of them are free from financial obligations and in search of a legitimating activity, they often take over the decision-making privilege of the trainer.

II

the
audience

5.

THE REGULARS

The audience is comprised of "regulars" and "occasionals." This is not an arbitrary division of participants, but a distinction recognized by the social actors. Regulars attend the race track as spectators on a day-to-day basis—that is, as long as their money holds out. Occasionals, by far the larger group, are those individuals who attend the race track once or twice a year, or as frequently as alternate Saturdays. The regulars *expect* to profit from their daily visits; the occasionals *hope* to profit. For the regulars, the race track is a way of life; for the occasionals, a form of recreation.

The major characteristic of the regulars is that they have largely dispelled the anxiety associated with the uncertainty and structured ambiguity of horse racing. They have succeeded in this either because they believe they have obtained a great quantity of information, because they believe they have worked out a sure-fire system, or because they believe they have access to authorities who are endowed with extraordinary shrewdness or inside information.

Perhaps the degree of uncertainty of a racing event can objectively be determined in some way. However, our concern is the degree of subjectively experienced uncertainty, and this varies widely from one race to another and from one player to another.[1]

1. For a good general statement see John Cohen, *Behavior in Uncertainty* (New York: Basic Books, 1964).

Most regulars bet heavily when they define a race's outcome as certain. But different categories of regulars will have varying degrees of uncertainty in the same situation, and different situations are socially defined as uncertain by different categories of regulars. This point will be returned to as we proceed with an elaboration of types of regulars.

The point that deserves emphasis here is that "serious" players will bet only in situations of subjective certainty. A complicating factor is that certainty and uncertainty exist on at least two levels. Moreover, the player can be certain (or uncertain) about the individual race or about his long-run success. In the following illustrations, I will be dealing only with certainty and uncertainty with respect to the individual race.

To begin with, a race's outcome can be defined as uncertain— and the player's belief in the uncertainty of the event can itself be certain. (Here the serious player will not bet, or make only a small bet.) The following interview [2] with a race track regular illustrates the point:

> *Interviewer*: Who do you like in this race?
> *Subject*: (Scrutinizing the *Racing Form*) Lord Victory looks like the best horse.
> *I*: Does he have a good chance?
> *S*: Well, it's really pretty much of an open race, but he's the best of the lot.
> *I*: How sure are you of that?
> *S*: You mean, how sure am I that this is a tough race? Oh, I'm sure of that. (The subject did not bet.)

The regular may define a race as uncertain, but be uncertain about his conviction of uncertainty:

> *I*: What looks good in this race?
> *S*: You just can't figure a race like this. [It was a 2-year-old maiden race, which is socially defined as being uncertain.] There's nothing you can really choose from.

2. These interviews might more properly be called "conversational encounters," since my presence at the track was taken by others as a normal part of the scene, that is, as an in-group regular.

I: Are you sure there's nothing good going here?
S: Well, actually Comiskey [a trainer] is pretty hot with first starters, and if the horse isn't washy [sweating heavily], he might jump out and steal the race. (The subject made a small bet.)

In the following interview, the subject was certain of the outcome, but doubtful of his certainty.

I: How does the race stack up?
S: Miller's Turk, wire to wire. He's the only thing in here with speed.
I: Then you're really going to lay in on this one?
S: Nope, the horse is too erratic, blows hot and cold.
I: Is there anything else in the race that looks good?
S: Can't see anything beating this horse. (The subject did not bet.)

Finally, the regular can be certain of the outcome and certain in his confidence in the outcome. Only here does the "serious" regular plunge heavily.

I: Who do you like?
S: No one, but no one beats the Diver.
I: How sure are you of that?
S: How sure? If he loses, I'll kiss your ass.

Let me point out again that even when the player is certain (at both confidence levels) of the outcome of the race, he cannot fully capitalize on this certainty. Not only would his own heavy betting affect the odds—the more bet, the less the payoff—but his betting activity would be communicated to others by the fluctuations on the tote board. Other players, seeing a precipitous decline in odds, would attribute this to the action of "smart money," starting a bandwagon effect and dropping the odds on a horse even more. (This system of self-destroying information thus serves as a kind of equilibrium mechanism by which a few insiders are prevented from excessively exploiting their information. By counteracting their activities somewhat, this mechanism helps maintain wider public participation in the game.)

While some players experience the sense of certainty with respect to a particular race, other players—the great majority of regulars—feel certain about the long-run turn of events. These players are not concerned with merely picking winners, but with betting an "overlay," a horse whose (subjective) probability of winning is greater than his odds (mutuel payoffs). The pursuit of the overlay has been described as "subjectively expected utility," or simply SEU. According to one student [3] of decision-making under conditions of uncertainty, individuals in risk-taking situations choose so as to maximize subjectively expected utility. Two independent concerns are involved: the value (or utility) of the prize and the probability of the outcome. In other words, individuals pursue a course of action that will give them the greatest prize and one that is most likely to materialize. Even if a player expects to lose a bet, the expected value of the play may be positive. For example, if the subjective probability of horse A is 2 to 1 and the odds are 5 to 1, and if the subjective probability of horse B is 1 to 1 and its odds are 1 to 1, the player will have greater expected value from horse A, even if he is more certain that horse B will win.[4] Because the decision of a player is in the direction of backing overlays, he tends to feel (in his betting) a sense of long-term certainty.

(While most players are making decisions in terms of the SEU model, the player who beats the game is the one whose subjective

3. Ward Edwards, "The Theory of Decision Making," *Psychological Bulletin*, 51 (1954), pp. 380–417. Two other papers by Edwards relevant to this discussion are "Probability-Preferences in Gambling," *American Journal of Psychology*, 66 (1953), pp. 349–364, and "The Prediction of Decisions among Bets," *Journal of Experimental Psychology*, 50 (1955), pp. 201–214.

4. In determining the expected value of his play, the bettor will take into consideration the morning line. The morning line, printed in the racing program, is the track handicapper's estimate of the probable odds of each horse in the race. If, for any given horse, the posted odds—that is, the odds that reflect the actual play of the crowd—are greater than that established on the morning line, many players will interpret this as a positive expected value. The horse with the greatest percentage increase, not the horse with the longest odds, will be seen by the regular as having the greatest positive subjective value. Thus a horse that is 2 to 1 on the morning line and has posted odds of 4 to 1 will have greater positive subjective value than a horse that is posted at 20 to 1 who was 8 to 1 on the morning line. For a player, the positive expected value of the first horse will be double that of the second horse.

probability of the outcome of a race is in accord with the objective probabilities. These objective probabilities, it will be argued, are themselves subjective. The complicated relation between subjective and objective probabilities and their relation to the problem of rationality will be examined in the appendix.)

Among the regulars that I have observed, I find few signs of anxiety resulting from uncertainty. If, as in the case of one type of player, he is uncertain at either the first or second stages of confidence, he doesn't bet (or makes a small token bet). Hence he has little or nothing at stake so as to cause anxiety. Another type of player, while uncertain about the particular race, is certain about his long-range success.

Perhaps because of this absence of subjective uncertainty, one finds—among most regulars at least—very little superstition or magic. As Devereux correctly observes:

> There seems to be far less superstition and magic connected with horse race gambling than there is associated with lotteries and with table games based upon pure chance. The basic reason for this is that horse race gambling offers considerably more scope for various skills and rational forms of orientation than do pure chance gambling situations. The race track gambler is not altogether helpless in determining a suitable course of action. He has wide ranges of choice, his success or failure is largely a result of these choices. . . . And thus it is that 'doping the races' presents both challenge and scope to rationally oriented gamblers who would not waste their time on a lottery or a game of dice.[5]

Although fans carry "lucky" objects (for example, baby teeth, mezuzahs, and the ever-popular rabbit's foot), their use as magical paraphernalia should not be exaggerated. For instance, one regular whose trademark was a battered brown fedora was asked if he thought his hat brought him luck. It turned out that he wore his "lucky" hat at the track because it was a good place to keep an "odds-percentage chart" to which he often referred in calculating probabilities. Another regular wore what he called his "good luck" tie. No, he didn't think it brought him luck—nor did he like wear-

5. Devereux, *op. cit.*, p. 622.

ing it—but his wife (who believed in luck) indicated that she would "give him hell" if he didn't wear it on racing days.

On the absence of magical practices, Devereux suggests:

> Whatever the inadequacies of his own knowledge and skills, the racing fan is aware, at least vaguely, that rational definitions are possible and that rational systems exist; indeed, if anything, the . . . race-goer is inclined to over-estimate the skills and scientific knowledge of the experts and "insiders." For these reasons, the fan is likely to blame his failures on his own lack of skill and knowledge, rather than upon ill-luck. And in this situation, frustration and anxiety tend to produce a different sort of adaptive behavior than direct resort to superstition and magic. Typically, he is inclined either to make some attempt to find a "rational" system for beating the races, or to surrender his own independence in a blind appeal to the judgment of some real or imputed authority.[6]

I might add that when the regular finds himself engaged in magical practices, he becomes anxious. If he should realize suddenly that he is himself jumping and shouting during a race to urge his selection home first, he will react to his own behavior with the disquiet of one who begins to see himself losing control. Magical practices, then, are anxiety-producing.[7] One of the characteristics of track regulars is their stolid observance of the race. This is another manifestation of the perceived character attribute of "coolness," highly valued by regulars. By maintaining his cool, the regular communicates to himself and others something about his style of life and the nature of his involvement in the particular event. Coolness, it appears, is a tribute the body makes to rationality. To lose one's cool is to lose one's sense.

The regular, then, comes to see himself as one who can *rationally* cope with the complexities of picking winners.

The Racing Form is crucial in the maintenance of the regular's self-concept as a rational speculator. This fact-filled document,

6. *Ibid.*, p. 623.
7. For a clear discussion of the relation between magic and anxiety, especially with respect to the theories of Malinowski and Radcliffe-Brown, see George C. Homans, *The Human Group* (New York: Harcourt, Brace, 1950), p. 321ff.

called the players' "bible," is a nationwide daily paper that carries news of racing, past performance charts, and results charts. Understanding the past and predicting future results are the perceived rewards for those men who religiously dedicate themselves to studying the "bible."

THE ADDICT

One type of regular deeply enmeshed in "bible" study is known as a "handicapper." From a psychoanalytic view, he might be called pathological because of his obsessional concern. From a certain sociological viewpoint, he might be called deviant in that his total involvement in the manipulation of figures has removed him from normal occupational and family role responsibilities. We will call such a player an "addict." Unfortunately, the term "addict" has value-laden implications (that is, businessmen with obsessional concerns about their financial activities are not regarded as addicts). The term "addict" in ordinary language also connotes a self-destructive compulsion. The compulsive player who continually loses at the game might more properly be called an "addict," but many of these "addicts" are beating the game. Because the term "handicapper," besides referring to a type of player, is also used to describe the racing secretary and the public newspaper selectors, I have chosen to use the term "addict" to describe a type of player whose standard orientation to the game involves a profound engrossment in the mechanical manipulation of figures.

Psychoanalysts, concerned with various forms of deviant behavior, have on occasion turned their attention to the compulsive gambler. Freud,[8] for instance, viewed the gambler as a sublimated masturbator; Bergler,[9] as a neurotic who expresses in his gambling a wish for self-destruction; Lindner,[10] as an "obsessional

8. "Dostoyevsky and Parricide," in *Collected Papers* (New York: Basic Books, 1959), 5, especially pp. 238ff.
9. Edmund Bergler, *The Psychology of Gambling* (New York: Hill and Wang, 1957).
10. Robert M. Lindner, "The Psychodynamics of Gambling," *Annals* (May 1950), p. 106.

neurotic engaged in what might be called the making of magic."

In discussing a race track addict's "moral career," my purpose is not to take issue with the various psychoanalytic conceptualizations, but to indicate that between, say, the urge to masturbate and the daily playing of horses lies a huge phenomenal reality that remains unexamined in the psychoanalytic literature.

By moral career, I refer to those significant stages that involve a shift in the individual's conception of self and others.[11]

In the first stage, the addict must come into contact with someone who has a familiarity with the racing scene and who can assist him in mastering the intricacies of reading the *Form*. Obviously, without such contacts, an individual cannot become a race track addict, though he might act out his "masturbatory tendencies" at the card table or in other forms of gambling. The following is part of an interview with a still-active addict. After quitting his job and turning to the race track as a full-time enterprise, his wife divorced him, blaming his horse-racing activities for the split. He explains how he got involved in racing:

I must of gone to the track maybe four or five times in my life before getting a job at Casey's [a liquor store]. I went with a friend who made the selections and we bet going in partners $5 apiece on each race. We lost each time, but had fun. My friend joined the army, and I never thought of going to the track for a while. But I kept up a little with racing news and was always interested in who won the Kentucky Derby. My friend made his selections from the *Form*, and once, when I thought I would go to the track myself, I bought a *Form* the night before and tried to read it. But it rained that day; so I didn't go to the track, and I didn't buy any *Forms* any more.

Then I got a job at Casey's and worked from four to midnight. They carried *Forms* there that came in about 8:30; that's when I first saw how excited people became over their bible. Boy, you should have seen the way those people acted when the *Form* was late and they had to stand around waiting. They'd turn to each other and ask, "What could have happened? Why is it late? Was there an accident?"

11. For a discussion of this concept see Goffman, *Asylums, op. cit.,* chapter 2.

Then they'd talk to each other about their common loss.
They'd begin to sweat, and ask me or the other liquor store
people to check out to see if they were carried in the other
stores. [Casey's is part of a chain.] Checking and rechecking
and all the while people acted like they faced a common
disaster. When the *Form* finally arrived, they'd make little
jokes like: "These *Forms* are as slow as the horses I bet."
By this time, the place would be so crowded with people
standing around that they'd be afraid that the *Forms* would be
all snatched up before they got theirs. So they'd start rushing and elbowing each other to get to the *Forms*. They'd try
to have fifty cents ready, so they could pull one off the top
and drop it down, rather than stand for change, where you
had to stand in line and wait your turn. If you dropped
even change, it was all right to grab.

Trainers and jockeys used to come in to buy *Forms*
there, but they never gave me any tips, except once—a
trainer who I caught stealing a five-cent candy bar gave me
the name of a horse. I looked at the *Form*, and, sure enough,
it was trained by the same man, at least they had the same
name according to his driver's license. The horse lost. But
I didn't bet it. Who would take a tip from a bum who'd
steal a five-cent candy bar?

We also had ticket sellers coming into the store. One of
them, a nice old man who I don't see around any more,
used to come in before closing and pick up his *Form*. He
asked me to put one aside for him each night, and I did. He
gave me a tip on a horse once, and it won at a fancy price.
I didn't bet the horse, but told him I did and asked him who
gave him the information. He said he picked it himself. He
did it two more times, and each time the horse won. The
third time I actually got someone to place a bet for me at the
track. I can't remember the name of the horse, but it paid
$11.80.

When business was slow, I would read the *Form* I put
aside for him and started making my own picks. I told him
what I liked, and he would tell me that the horses I picked
didn't stand a chance or weren't worth betting because of
the odds. He showed me some of the things to look for in
the *Form*. This went on for about a month. Then the horses
went south, and I didn't see him around. But we still got
the *Form*, and I started following the horses myself. I got
a book that also explained a lot to me.

When I would get home, my wife would be waiting up
for me, watching television. But instead of going to bed
with her, I would sit up the night and make my selections.
I couldn't wait for the results. I started doing pretty good.
I was doing better than Sweep [a selector in the *Form*],

and it was a thrill to pick a horse that Sweep had called "Has shown little" and see it win.

Because I worked the night shift, it was easy to get to the track for a few races and come back in time for work. At first I didn't do too hot, barely breaking even. But by the end of the season, I had won about $700 and hid it from my wife. She knew I was going to the track occasionally, but since I was never broke and brought home the steady pay check, she didn't ask any questions. When the horses went south, I found a bookie. He ran a dry cleaning store as a front. He was a louse bookie who would shit in his pants if you bet more than $10 on a horse. Anyway, I clipped him with a $20 bet that paid $54.60, and he gave me back $420 [Bookies typically pay only 20-1 maximum]. He said he didn't want my business any more.

By this time, I had $2,000 in winnings and savings. I called the store and told them I was sick and drove down south where the horses were running. I told my wife I would be back in a few days, but she screamed at me anyway and didn't really know what I was up to. I got there on a Wednesday and came back on Sunday with more than $5,000. Instead of being thrilled my wife cried and said she hated me. I quit the store and left my wife and went back south. I've been playing the ponies ever since.

Thus, in the first stage of his moral career, the addict comes to learn the intricacies of handicapping and mastery of the factual information to be found in the *Form*. Success in handicapping and the tangible evidence of cashing bets and making money indicate to the player that he has indeed obtained some degree of mastery.

A higher level of participation—the second stage of the addict's moral career—occurs as soon as the player sees himself as one who can rationally cope with the complexities of picking a winner. By "rationally cope" I refer to two related, but independent components of the player's belief system. The first component involves the player perceiving a race as a natural event, ordered and capable of being determined by analysis. To maintain this belief, the player need only be able to give a reasonable account as to why the horse that he selected lost, and why the horse that finished first won. Reasonable accounts as to why his horse—presumably a fit and ready animal—lost are easy to come by: the distance of the race was a little too long or a little too short; the condition of the track was slightly off, or too hard; the cinch was too tight or too loose; the horse's shoe was thrown or too tight; his recent workout was too stiff, or not stiff enough; he didn't like the blinker change (on or off); he was pressed too soon on the lead, or wasn't pressed enough; he didn't like the way the jockey rode him; he sulked at the whip; he was carried wide, forced against the rail, bumped, or tripped on the heels of another horse; he was caught flat-footed at the break; his saddle slipped; he got scared by his shadow and tried to jump over it and lost stride; he was shaken by the noise of the crowd. And so on.

Accounting for a loser is easy; explaining why the horse that won—but wasn't bet—was playable is only slightly more involved. In this regard, the *Racing Form* is very likely to serve a function similar to that of the poison oracles reported by Evans-Pritchard in his work on the beliefs of the Azande.[12] An oracle-poison (extracted from a creeper and given to a fowl) becomes, according to Zande belief, effective after appropriate incantation. Questions posed to the poison oracle are answered in terms of the effects of the poison on the fowl. In response to the same question, the oracle can successively answer Yes or No. This is not taken as a contradiction by the Azande. Rather the natives "rationally" account for the discrepancy by insisting that the wrong variety of poison was used or some taboo spoiled the poison, and so on. In other words, no matter what the outcome, the Azande can "rationally" interpret the events.[13]

In a similar fashion, the addict finds an interpretation in a contradictory pattern and in this way explains any occurrence. Of course, he uses the *Racing Form* instead of poison oracles. Therefore, a horse won because it was recently raced ("That proves he was in condition") or not raced in some time ("The trainer freshened his animal with a rest and so it won at first asking"); because it had fast workouts ("The horse was primed in the morn-

12. E. E. Evans-Pritchard, *Witchcraft, Oracles and Magic Among the Azande* (Oxford: The Clarendon Press, 1937).

13. That this form of "rationality" is not restricted to the Azande but constitutes a routine mechanism in constructing the social world is amply demonstrated by Harold Garfinkel. See "Commonsense Knowledge of Social Structure," *op. cit.*

ing") or slow workouts ("The trainer didn't want the horse to run his race in the morning") ; because the horse dropped weight ("The trainer tipped his intentions") or picked up weight ("The trainer found an easy spot for a repeat win"). In short, an item— or its opposite—may serve as a warrant to account for the outcome of the race.[14]

As the addict sees it, with each race an increment is added to his stock of knowledge, which in turn makes the racing world meaningful and sustains his belief in the rationality of the game. Paradoxically, every losing bet merely confirms the potentiality of the rational selection of a continual string of winners. *Therefore, through a process of ratiocination, the addict sees himself as picking the winner of every race.* This might be related to the sense of omnipotence Lindner reports as characteristic of the gambler.[15]

The second component of the notion of "rationally coping" is a verbal rationalization that the activity the addict is engaged in is not gambling, but is "business." By calling his activities "business" the addict justifies his day-to-day attendance at the track, and what would be considered a deviant way of life is thus made legitimate.

In his analysis of the professional gambler, Morehead remarks that "the habitual compulsive gambler is relatively rare, the occasional compulsive gambler quite common." [16] I am suggesting here that once the player comes to legitimate his activity as being a business, his compulsive gambling becomes habitual.

In the final stage of an addict's moral career, he becomes enmeshed in a web of relations with other addicts. Because of their daily attendance, and because of a race track norm that permits individuals to have easy access to each other (for example, one can approach a stranger and ask who he likes in a race and be

14. These are in fact good reasons in explaining the outcome of the race, and among those addicts who are beating the game such accounts are probably in accord with the objective realities. My point, however, is that the contradictory pattern of "reasons" facilitates the addict in invoking a "reasonable" account, which in turn has the consequence of maintaining the stability of his belief in the rationality of the game.

15. Lindner, *op. cit.,* p. 106.

16. Albert H. Morehead, "The Professional Gambler," *Annals, op. cit.,* p. 84.

certain to get an answer), the addicts tend to find each other. Teaming up with others, the addict can not only learn and discuss new ideas of manipulating data and other shared interests (for example, how to beat the income tax laws), but also learn certain attitudes and rationalizations that confirm his image of being a "free" man while at the same time being engaged in a legitimate business. In my observation, these friendships cut across class and racial lines.[17] Racing addicts recognize themselves as people with a common fate.

Thus, race track addicts make up a quasi-group (with its members moving in and out) whose few membership qualifications are daily attendance, the mastery of a technical race track jargon, and a front of restraint and self-discipline. With respect to this last criterion, one conducts himself in a businesslike fashion, giving the appearance of "affective neutrality." For the addict, the maintenance of affective neutrality means one doesn't lose his cool. The exercise of such expressive control validates that one is rationally engaged in a business.

The norms governing the interaction of addicts are: never pry into the background and external activities of another player (unless these are in some way related to horse racing, such as how one handles the problem of income tax); and, never push an individual to divulge secrets of data manipulation; information is freely given, or not given at all. However, reciprocity with regard to information is common; a you-tell-me-your-secrets-and-I'll-tell-you-mine attitude prevails. Another bond between the addicts is their shared evaluation of the betting public as a pack of boobs, and they feel that success in betting is attained easily because their competition is so uninformed.

The community of addicts serves a tension-management func-

17. It does not appear, however, that these friendships extend beyond the track. The external life of race track regulars is a subject yet to be explored. It would be of interest to know, for instance, about the involvement of regulars in the kinship and occupational structure. Because of the race track norm prohibiting inquiry into the player's external life, I felt constrained from asking such questions. Had I made such inquiries in my role as apparent member, my actions would have appeared "strange." In seven cases I have relevant but fragmentary data, insufficient to warrant any generalizations.

tion for the player in a slump. The support comes by way of an expressed ideology that the crowd is always wrong. If the addict is in a slump, it is only temporary—because he is not part of the public and so long as he bets against the public he will succeed.

Since the public's choice is by definition the favorite, one seldom finds the addicts playing favorites. A man who consistently plays favorites is called a "chalk eater" and is an object of ridicule. The rule is "copper the public," that is, play against it. But the concern of the addict is not to fish for long shots, but to obtain an overlay, which is, as suggested earlier, a horse whose probability of winning is greater than his odds.

In closing this discussion of the addict culture, let me point out one norm that is so inviolate that it constitutes a taboo: No player is to inquire as to the *amount* of money bet on a selection. Inquiring about another player's selection is permissible and even, to some degree, about the means of reaching his decision, but never the amount he will play. Not only is the amount played not mentioned, but because of the structural arrangements at the track, the exact amount bet is not observed by others. In other public forms of gambling—roulette, blackjack, craps—the player's betting is an observable feature of the event. Under this condition, he is subject to being egged on by observers. Thus the craps player sometimes finds himself directing his betting for the benefit of an audience, which will evaluate his moral character in terms of his willingness to keep the dice rolling and letting the wad ride.[18] The horse player, on the other hand, can maintain a more rational control over his betting.

In horse rooms or bookie establishments, the player is often in the same situation as the casino gambler—both having audiences to witness betting—and this is one of the reasons for the success of the house. Zola's account of horse-race gambling in an establishment known as Hoff's place indicates the pressures placed on a gambler by the audience and the manner in which he is egged on to increase his bets,[19] resulting in his failure to beat the bookie. (Betting with a bookie will be discussed in a later chapter.)

18. Goffman, "Where the Action Is," *op. cit.*
19. Irving K. Zola, "Observations on Gambling in a Lower-Class Setting," in H. S. Becker (Ed.), *The Other Side* (New York: Free Press of Glencoe, 1964), pp. 247–260.

BIG-TIME GAMBLERS

Racing lore is rich with the names of famous gamblers. There was Chicago O'Brien, who originated the system of betting the favorite for show. He was reputed to have bet $100,000 on Man o' War at odds of 1 to 100, and thus won $1,000 for that investment. His school of playing is still popular.

A second school of playing developed from the methods of the underworld financier Arnold Rothstein. His style was to fix races. Followers of this method, though recognizing that fixed races are a phenomenon of a nostalgic past, emphasize the importance of *inside* (or *hot*) *information*. They try to obtain first-hand information about the betting operations of horsemen.

The Pros

While Chicago O'Brien and Arnold Rothstein were known as gamblers, they played only "sure" things, based either on small-risk systems or inside dope. The style of play of today's pros evolves from Pittsburgh Phil, who maintained that successful gambling involves betting on overlays, selected on the basis of a variety of types of information.

Pittsburgh Phil's method had two key aspects: the study of past performances and the observational gleaning of trainers' intentions. Since Phil operated before past performance charts, he made his own, for which he had to rely on memory. "I can recall," he once remarked, "a long-passed race vividly, every detail of it, the weights carried, the distance, the condition of it and every incident that happened during the running." [20] These "amazing" feats of memory actually are commonplace among betting regulars.[21] But Phil took this skill out of the realm of enjoyable nostalgia and applied it for profit.

According to Phil:

20. Cole, *op. cit.*
21. The relation between memory and occupational interest is discussed in F. C. Bartlett, *Remembering* (Cambridge University Press, 1932).

The racing man should arise in the morning, cool and clear-
headed, and with the first opening of his eyes he should
again take up the problem of the day. The horses come
before him at once, and they never leave until after the
contest is decided. I think about them the very first thing
when I awaken, weighing them in one light and from one
standpoint and another. As I dress and eat my breakfast,
I am placing them here and there, giving each a chance
until at last from all standpoints I decide which one, in a
truly and perfectly run race, devoid of the hundred or more
unlooked for incidents that can happen, should be the
winner.[22]

Phil's account demonstrates that study and evaluation of
horses can occupy almost all of one's time. And the time thus
spent removes one from conventional role obligations, one of the
common features of the handicapper-addict and the pro.[23]

While the moral career of the handicapper-addict and the
pro is essentially the same, their methods and financial success
differ. The handicapper relies solely on data manipulation. The
pro, following still another side of Phil's methodology, is unquestionably the more successful of the two: His success stems from
his concern with the study of horsemen as well as horses. Thus
Phil advised that "the man who would be successful should be
able not only to know his horses, but to know the methods of
those who were engaged in the direct control of the horses." [24]

Remember that the trainer is not always trying to win; the
pro, realizing this, must in some manner be able to unravel the
trainer's intentions. Remember, too, that the trainer maintains a
secretiveness about his plans. How, then, may the intentions of
the trainer be gleaned?

Phil suggested his own procedure when he remarked: "What
may appear to be right on paper, very, very often is wrong in

22. Cole, *op. cit.,* pp. 25–26.
23. Morehead writes: "In the case of some games, so profound that
their science is capable of challenging any intellect, the ambition to
master the game becomes an obsession. Since the study requires all one's
time and more, the addict finds it difficult to make a living by conventional pursuits and saves as much time as he needs to devote to his study"
(*op. cit.,* p. 83).
24. Cole, *op. cit.,* p. 8.

the paddock." [25] While handicappers and other regulars visit the paddock before the race to size up the horse, the pro goes there to size up the trainer. The pro knows the paddock is the one place where the trainer *must* disclose his intentions. Moreover, the paddock is not a backstage arena, but one of the showplaces of the race track open to the public.

Before receiving instructions in the paddock, the jockey does not know the trainer's intentions. Even if the jockey will ride several mounts for the same stable on the same day, the trainer will not let him know his plans (for fear of an information leak) until those final few minutes in the paddock before the race. Because the trainer withholds his designs until the last moment, his intentions are tipped publicly rather than disclosed secretively under candlelight behind the barn door; the paddock has no barn door to hide behind. For these reasons, the pro need not worry about created appearances, but can take the actions of the trainer and jockey at face value.

Of course, the trainer's unmasked intentions are not patently obvious. Rather, one must learn how to read what goes on in the paddock.

The pro keeps a sharp eye on the trainer and jockey as they huddle in the stall; for every movement might be a telltale sign. If, while receiving instructions from the trainer, the jockey has an inattentive gaze and appears to be inner-absorbed, or if his interest is partially engaged with the activities of others in the paddock, the pro strongly suspects that the trainer is telling him: "Don't push the horse." On the other hand, if the trainer is "shooting," he may remove his program from his pocket, give lengthy instructions to the jockey and point to the names of the horses in that race that are dangerous competitors. In looking for tipoffs, the pro searches for elements of incongruity. In his long association with racing, the pro has developed a sensitivity to slight variations in paddock behavior. In time, he notices that certain things stand out from the ordinary. Knowing the typical behavior of the trainer allows the pro to infer what the former has in mind—and to bet accordingly.

25. *Ibid.,* p. 27.

Sharpshooters

The paradigm of the sharpshooter was Chicago O'Brien, who emphasized the sure-thing bet. Sharpshooters—no risk, or small-risk players—may be categorized as follows:

The Bridge Jumper. The bridge jumper is the no-risk, ultraconservative player who makes large bets on hot favorites for show. Laws in most states that permit parimutuel betting stipulate that the track return a minimum payoff of five to ten cents to the dollar. Therefore, the player who bets, say, $5,000 for show is guaranteed by law a $500 profit. Because of "bridge jumping," hot favorites in small fields sometimes create a minus pool (that is, so much money has been placed on a horse that the track has to make up the state minimum out of its own pocket).

The expression "bridge jumper" refers to a race track belief that if a player has had many no-risk successes, he will put an end to it all at the first setback. The expression is very popular and when an odds-on (less than 1 to 1) favorite in a small field runs out of the money, the racing news will say: "It was a bad day today for the bridge jumpers."

The bridge jumper must play at the track, which is one of the reasons he is a regular. Bookies will not accept bets on show alone. If a player wishes to make a show bet with a bookie, he must also play the horse for win and place. If the bridge jumper can get a bookie to take his bets, he may opt to do so. Other sure-thing players—the "dutcher" and the "bellringer" —have no such option. Their whole style of play involves capitalizing on the resources of the track itself.

The Dutcher. The dutcher bets every horse in a race except one and wins a predetermined amount on each investment no matter which horse wins—unless, of course, the winner is the one horse not played. The key to the dutcher's operation is his familiarity with the table of "equivalent percentages," what he calls the "book" (the total of all the betting percentages in a race). The betting percentage of any set of odds is, by definition, equal to the nearest "extension" to 100. The idea of "betting percentage" is clearly understood once the notion of the "extension" is clarified.

An extension is the amount a player gets back including his own money. For instance, if the player bets $2 on a 2-to-1 shot, his extension is $6—his $4 winnings plus his original $2 bet. The extension then nearest to 100 for a 2-to-1 shot would be $33; for $33 bet on a 2-to-1 shot would return $99—$66 winnings plus the $33. Thus, the equivalent percentage of a 2-to-1 shot is 33 per cent. By similar reasoning, a 4-to-1 shot is 20 per cent.

By definition, a book equals 100 per cent. A race with five horses each at 4 to 1 would make up a book. If a player bet $2 on every horse in this race, he would break even no matter which horse won. That is, his total investment would be $10, and no matter which horse won, the return would be $10. Suppose, however, that one of these horses was 9 to 1. Since the equivalent percentage of a 9-to-1 shot is 10 per cent, then the total of this race is 90 per cent—the four horses at 20 per cent (at 4 to 1) and one horse at 10 per cent (at 9 to 1). This is known as a "dutch" book.

Now if the player bets $20 on each of the 4-to-1 shots, and $10 on the 9-to-1 shot, then no matter which horse wins, the player must show a $10 profit. Whenever one finds a dutch book— one less than 100 per cent—he cannot lose. In the days before parimutuel betting, when bookmakers set up their operations openly at the track, a dutch bettor could win every race he played —if he were quick enough. For instance, if bookie A was receiving heavy play on a certain horse, he would cut its price and raise the odds of all the other contenders. Meanwhile, if bookie B was being played heavily on another horse, he would cut those odds and raise others. Thus as soon as a line of bookmakers had less than 100 per cent, a bettor could wager on every horse in the race in proportion to the equivalent percentages and win no matter which horse finished first.

Today, one can no longer dutch the bookmakers, since they do not determine the odds; rather the bookmakers' payoffs are determined by the track odds. Nor can one beat the track, since the odds are automatically figured to ensure, not only a round book (of 100 per cent), but what gamblers call a "winning book" (of 110 or 115 per cent, the percentage over 100 being the track take). For instance, if the track take is 10 per cent, one might find in a six-horse race five horses at 4 to 1 and one horse at 9 to 1. Since the percentage equivalent of a 4-to-1 shot is 20 per cent and a 9-to-1 shot is 10 per cent, then the book equals 110 per cent. Hence in every race the track would pocket 10 per cent, and the other 100 per cent would be distributed to the holders of the winning tickets. Since play with the bookie is distributed similarly to the play at the track, the bookie is assured of a 10 per cent profit. However, while the track in principle (except where there is a minus pool) must always make 10 to 15 per cent on every race, the bookie in principle can lose on every race. But, as we shall later see, the bookie's take is typically far greater than the track take.

The dutcher today operates in the following manner: He waits for a race where he has information that the favorite will not win (which occurs 70 per cent of the time). For instance, suppose the dutcher learns that a horse, though having good recent form, has become unsound and that the trainer will be dropping the horse down in class in hopes that someone will claim it. Suppose now it is a seven-horse race. The horse with recent form and dropping down will surely be at least an even-money favorite (that is, odds of 1 to 1, or 50 per cent). The other six horses, let us say, are 9 to 1, or 10 per cent each, equalling 60 per cent. Since the track take is 10 per cent, then the book equals 110 per cent. (Again, no matter who wins the race, the track must make 10 per cent on the race.) Now here is the key to the dutcher's operation: He ignores the even-money horse and plays, say, $100 on each of the remaining horses. His total investment is $600. No matter which horse wins, he must show a profit of $400.

A variation of this operation is to throw out the second-choice horse. But the key move is always the same: to throw out one horse in order to create a dutch book that guarantees a profit no matter which of the other horses win. While other players are concerned with picking winners, the dutcher seeks information on losers.

To locate losing horses, the dutcher need not rely on inside information. Rather he keeps lists of trainers that *never* try the first time out at a new track, horses that refuse to extend themselves on muddy tracks, and trainers who drop a "form" horse down in class *only* when their animals have become unsound and thus have no chance of winning. While the bridge jumper must live with the fear that a mishap will put his bet out of the money, the dutcher—because of the virtual certainty of his operation—may play a lifetime without ever losing a bet. For the dutcher to lose, a mishap must afflict all the horses. The confidence of the dutcher is expressed in his proneness not to watch the race, but to move from the seller's window to the cashier's window and to tantalize the puzzled cashier with the statement: "Don't worry, buddy. I got this one in the bag." [26]

The Bellringer. The bellringer is someone who seeks to make a wager *after* the horses have left the starting gate.

After the starter releases the horses from the gate, he then pushes a second button that locks the mutuel machines. The interim between the period when the horses leave the gate and the machines lock is six to ten seconds. Now six seconds isn't much time, but considering that the average race is seventy seconds, and one-fifth of a second is equal to one length, it is clear that a player can get down a bet while the horses have run some thirty lengths or one-eighth of a mile (or one furlong).

Bellringing demands team effort and split-second timing. The bellringer stations himself at the $100 window when the horses have entered the starting gate. At the start, after two or three seconds have elapsed, the partner signals which horse has broken on top and the bellringer slaps down $100 or buys as many tickets as possible until the mutuel machine locks. This is not an illegal activity, but merely a way of "working" the system.

Bellringers generally restrict themselves to sprint races, and

26. We might reiterate here that the amount the dutcher plays on each horse depends on its odds; thus he must play at the track where he can use the resources of the tote board that flashes changes in the odds. At the bookie joint, he is bereft of such knowledge.

preferably to 2-year-old races where the distance is as short as two furlongs. In these short races, the horse that jumps out in the lead has a tremendous advantage, and the bellringer finds himself backing virtual sure things. But even in longer races, the bell-ringer can correctly estimate those situations where, if a certain horse can "break out on top," he won't be headed. Also a hot- and cold-running horse may indicate its good form by breaking out in front. At the very least, the bellringer can be assured that his play got away well from the gate and hasn't suffered the type of mishap that very often puts horses out of contention from the outset.

The Insider

The insider's play is wholly dependent on what he takes to be hot information (that is, trainers' tips). Success obviously depends upon the insider's ability to make and maintain contacts with horsemen. In turn, this success depends on what he has to trade for reliable information. The insider of course may bet $50 or more for a trainer. But he will avoid this policy; for his routine operation is to contact two or three trainers in a race, and it is unprofitable to buy tickets for all of them. More often what he trades upon is friendship. Most inside men are former horsemen who rely on personal ties to gain information from active horse-men. Usually these inside men are close to being down-and-outers, and information is given to them more out of charity than any-thing else. But in obtaining this information, the insider must time precisely the moment to inquire as to the trainer's intentions. The closer to post time, the more candid the trainer's response. Thus to get a reliable tip, the insider will approach the trainer just minutes before the race, which, of course, severely limits the number of trainers he can contact for any given race. By struc-turing social relations, time thwarts the achievement of goals.

Frequently, the insider enters into a partnership with a backer who will give him money to bet on a 50-50 split. Thus, the insider exchanges his involvement in a web of relationships among horse-men for capital. In this arrangement, the insider runs no risk, but he must produce. The backer—since he is not informed until *after* the race what the insider played—assumes that his contact will "finagle" (or welsh) some bets, and thus he is excessively demanding as to the continual production of winners and profits.

Because of this assortment of pressures, the insider seldom succeeds for long in his operation. A role that clearly indicates failure in the game, the insider is usually the last rung on a downward ladder. The next step is complete abandonment of racing.

DISCREPANT ROLES

Among the track regulars are a number of other individuals whose vantage point is either clearly illegitimate (that is, deviant) or in some way marginal to the on-going action. These individuals occupy what will be called "discrepant roles." [27]

Legitimate Roles

The Press. On every daily newspaper, the sportswriters are considered a separate breed. Not only are they ecologically removed from the other reporters (the sports department is almost always separated from other news departments), but they operate with special codes of their own. They shun the $5WH$ lead (the (who-what-where-when-why-and-how lead) for the narrative; they permit themselves the biases of reporting that boost the home teams, and they freely mix reporting with editorial comment. A sportswriter is expected to handle all kinds of sporting events. However, if a newspaper is located in a racing area, it will hire one man whose specialty is horse racing. Horse racing is considered a sport *sui generis*, and the talents required here do not overlap with the reporting and coverage of other sports. Moreover, a paper's racing man will also be called upon to make daily selections at the local track—a skill no journalism school teaches. While a newspaper generally expects superior *writing* from its

27. The term is taken from Goffman's *Presentation of Self, op. cit.,* chapter 4.

sports writers (note they are called "writers"; most other staff
members covering news are called reporters), the paper expects
superior *selections* from its man on the track beat.

In the track press box then, we find the men whose selections
are open to public scrutiny. They believe that their jobs and their
papers' circulation will depend to some degree on their ability to
pick winners. Because they must make selections for every race
(under deadline conditions) before they can see the past performance charts, the newspaper selectors must rely on their own horse-
index files. These files contain a minimal amount of information,
and so selections are based on "sight" picks, hunches, and wild
guesses. For this reason, the men in the press box sometimes refer
to their domain as the "psycho ward," or "mad house." "Mad-
ness," as the men in the press box put it, "is being forced to make
a decision without sufficient information."

Along with the local newspaper representatives, the press box
will include at least two men from the *Racing Form* who are known
as chart callers. Their comments and observations are reported as
part of the results charts printed the following day in the *Form*.
Here is a sample:

> MARTIN'S ARK, in close attendance to the pace, assumed com-
> mand from the outside on the final bend, was briefly headed
> in the last sixteenth and, responding to strong handling,
> came again to outfinish FAIRMAR. The latter, unhurried
> when outrun early, was sent to the outside when commencing
> his rally on the final turn and, continuing his response,
> forged to the front in the last sixteenth and narrowly missed.
> BUTTERMILK PIKE, always formidable, saved ground through-
> out and lacked the necessary closing rally. JUST PLAIN LUCKY
> failed to menace. WINISTED could not keep up. OVER CURRENT
> displayed speed for five furlongs and gave way.

The *Racing Form* also stations at every track a force of espionage agents, known as "clockers." Their job is to spy on horses
and report their workouts. At daybreak, the clockers appear in
the grandstands and begin taking notes and often keep three
watches going at the same time. They must recognize every horse
on sight. How they do this is something of a mystery, but to hear

a clocker tell it: "To me, all people look alike; only horses are different." To simplify the task of identifying horses, the clockers make use of a complicated identification system that involves distinctive colorings and markings (known as snips, stars, blazes, stockings, etc.), as well as designations for types of manes and tails. As soon as these are learned, no horse escapes the watchful eyes of the clockers, and all workouts are reported in the *Form*.

Unless a trainer works his horses before daybreak ("by oil lamp," as the expression goes), he must assume that the clocker will be able to identify his animals. What the clocker doesn't know is the pole the trainer will use to begin the horse's work. The shrewd trainer will work three horses together and break each of them at the same time at different poles. In this manner, the trainer hopes that the clocker will not catch all the horses in their actual trials and will have a false clocking, or perhaps no clocking at all. These maneuvers are especially important in the case of the 2-year-old whose true ability the trainer wishes to disguise. In this century-old contest between trainers and clockers, trainers reluctantly admit that they usually lose the covering-and-uncovering game—unless they rely on such devious tactics as the predawn workout and changing the markings of the horse (for instance, putting shoe polish on a horse's white blaze).

The Stooper. The stooper makes his living by picking up all discarded betting tickets and cashing redeemable tickets at the window. In a fifty-day meet, the value of uncashed tickets genererally runs $51,000, or an average of about $1,000 per day.[28] Undoubtedly, the figure would be higher were it not for the stooper.

A major source of uncashed tickets comes from those people who don't know they have a winning ticket. For instance, some players who bet a horse for place or show believe that unless the horse runs second or third (respectively), they have a losing bet. Of course, if a horse is played for place and it comes in first or second, the player collects the place price; if a horse is played for show and it runs first, second, or third, the holder receives the show price. As a rule, the place price is about one half the win

28. Ernest E. Blanche, *Off to the Races* (New York: A. S. Barnes, 1947), p. 98.

price, and the show price about a third the win price. Thus a mutuel of, say, $12 win, $6 place, and $4 show is perceived as normal.

Another source of discards comes from the player who unthinkingly asks for a number he did not intend to play or who gets a number he didn't request. When these players don't look at the parimutuel ticket, they may assume that they have lost their bet and drop their tickets after the race. Players frequently report the reverse situation: They think they have won the race only to see that the tickets they hold bear the number of another horse.

A final source of discards occurs after the horses have passed the finish line but before the race is declared official. As soon as the race is over, the stooper starts looking for discarded win tickets on the horse that finished second and for discarded place tickets on the horse that finished third. If a horse is disqualified, the stooper will be holding live tickets. Despite the public address announcer's continual reminder not to destroy parimutuel tickets until the results of the race are declared official, most players discard their presumably losing tickets immediately after the horses pass the finish line (except where their selections are involved in a photo finish).

Stoopers who are sensitive about the raised eyebrows that often greet an adult engaged in the "occult involvement" [29] of stooping will frequently bring their children to the track to pick up tickets. What is an occult involvement for an adult is a normal activity for a child.

Lady Bountiful. A race track has three areas of observation, associated with three classes of fans: the grandstand, for the working class; the club house, for the middle class; and the turf club, for the upper class. The average prices of admission for these areas are $1.50, $2.50, and $4.50, respectively. About 75 per cent of the crowd is in the grandstand, another 20 per cent in the club house, and 5 per cent in the turf club. Here in the elegant, country-club atmosphere of the turf club sits Lady Bountiful, not for

29. On "occult involvements," see Goffman, *Behavior in Public Places, op. cit,* p. 76.

the purpose of playing the races but displaying the wealth and style of her social position.[30]

Officially the turf club is a public place, a location "where the general cultural definition permits many people from many diverse categories to be present for varying periods of time and often for varying reasons." However, Lady Bountiful regards the turf club as a "home territory," where she has—as at her home—a sense of intimacy, freedom, and control.[31]

With her friends, Lady Bountiful stakes out a certain area at the turf club. She knows that by going to this area she will find her other daily companions. During the course of the day, these women will lunch on duck l'orange, sip Manhattans and occasionally leave their table to place a $2 bet. When new faces appear to invade the territory, they will be stared at; and if the new figures are not suitably accoutered in high fashion, they will be stared down. That these women regard the turf club as a home territory is indicated by the fact that when placing a bet all the occupants of a table may leave their handbags unattended. I know of no other public area where women do this. During the race, the conversation at the tables may continue uninterrupted, the race being a backdrop for other types of activity.

Illegal Operators

So far, I have been discussing legitimate discrepant roles. We now turn to an array of illegal roles, the most spectacular being the pastposter, a man who plays the races after they are run.[32] Obviously he doesn't bet at the track.

The Pastposter. Pastposting is always a team operation in-

---

30. Other turf club regulars are owners, trainers, and officials. The occasionals here consist of high rollers, celebrities, and a category that can best be descibed as cute-young-things-on-the-make.

31. Sherri Cavan, *Liquor License* (Chicago: Aldine Publishing Company, 1966), chapter 10.

32. For an account of past posting and its relation to the con game known as "the pay-off," see David W. Maurer, *The Big Con* (Signet Books, 1962).

volving at least three members. One man is stationed at the track and signals the results; a second, at a phone booth; and a third, in a bookie joint. The success of this operation depends upon two factors: first, that the bookie joint accepts bets up to the moment it receives the results on the "wire," and second, that the information received by the operator in the bookie joint arrives before the bookie receives the wire information. The latter is usually possible because the race results first go to a central office and then relayed to the local bookie joints.

To avoid being pastposted, bookies try to deal only with clients that have, in the bookie jargon, "no snow on their shoes" (persons who can be trusted because they have been sitting in the joint long enough for the snow to have melted from their shoes). When operating with a suspecting bookie, the pastposters add a fourth man, who signals the information to the "dry-shoed" member. The system operates as follows:

The horses have just crossed the finish line and the man at the track—if he is using modern equipment—relays the information by walkie-talkie to the man in an off-track phone booth (race tracks have no public phones), who is already on the line with a third member outside the bookie joint. Meanwhile, the dry-shoed operator is studying the *Form* (appearing in deep concentration) and talking to the bookie, telling him he can't make up his mind which horse to bet and whether or not he should drop his whole wad or quit for the day. His man enters and flashes a signal across the room. "Is it too late to make a bet?" the dry-shoed player asks. "No," says the bookie, "but you'd better hurry." "Okay," replies the operator, "the hell with it. Here's the whole bundle on No. 10." A minute later, the bookie gets the results: No. 10 is the winner at a fancy price, and he is left wondering whether he has been taken by an outfit of pastposters.

The Pigeon Passer. A pigeon is a losing or counterfeit parimutuel ticket that the passer attempts to get cashed. A common maneuver is to attempt to palm off discarded losing tickets. After picking up discarded losing tickets of various denominations and numbers, the pigeon passer waits for a horse to win with a number corresponding with that of one of these tickets. The trick in cashing the ticket is in selecting the right kind of cashier. The successful pigeon passer is a specialist in identifying inexperienced or easily intimidated cashiers.

Winning ticket holders—especially of the lower denominations —are impatient to collect. The inexperienced cashier fears he is not distributing the payoffs fast enough. When the passer presents his pigeons, he hopes that the cashier will simply glance at the winning number and redeem the tickets. When the paid tickets reach the ticket checker, the pigeons are discovered. The price of these tickets are charged to the cashier.[33] Since the inexperienced cashier is the most vulnerable victim of the pigeon passer, the former usually is assigned the cashier's window of the lowest denomination.

One variation of this method is to slip in a pigeon along with legitimate tickets. Suppose the passer buys a $10 ticket in the first race on horse No. 1, which loses. In the third race, he again bets the horse in post position No. 1, perhaps buying two $10 tickets. If No. 1 wins, the passer will attempt to palm off the pigeon from the first race along with the two winning tickets. When the cashier is presented with three tickets, he is likely to study the first one only for correctness and merely glance at the others, thus assuming their legitimacy. If a pigeon is detected, the passer can claim ignorance (a mistake was made; how foolish of him; sorry, he must have thrown away the good tickets by mistake). When a pigeon is accompanied by legitimate tickets, the passer is assured of not being apprehended for his chicanery.

A more reckless enterprise involves passing counterfeit tickets. Here the scheme is to pick up discarded losing tickets and treat them so that their illegitimacy cannot be detected by sight nor touch. The counterfeiter will take a $50 ticket and carefully peel off the portion identifying the race and the accompanying code symbols. Then, on a ticket bearing the mutuel number of a winning horse, he applies the proper race identification. This operation can be done quickly, and the treated ticket will get through even the most experienced cashier.

33. Fred S. Buck, *Horse Race Betting* (New York. Greenberg, 1046), pp. 49–50.

To prevent this activity, tickets are from time to time placed before an ultraviolet light (located next to the cashier's cage), which detects altered tickets. The cashier will flash a ticket in front of the ultraviolet light if the person holding the ticket looks suspicious. The cashier is expected to be an occupational specialist in judging the moral character of the players from their appearance. When one of these treated pigeons is detected, the cashier immediately reports the incident via a radio transmitter alerting one of the track policemen to pick up the pigeon passer.

To avoid being picked up, the pigeon passer may sober up a skid-row type and hire his services for the day to cash a series of doctored tickets. An alternative procedure used by the passer is to go to a railroad station to sell the treated tickets to people headed for the track by train. He indicates to a likely prospect by pointing to the program of the day before that the No. 2 horse won the last race and the payoff is over $60, but he had to leave before cashing in and—because he can't get to the track today—he will sell the ticket for $50.

The Tout. As a verb, "tout" refers to the suggesting of a winner on the basis of inside information or expertise. The term, however, is always used in some derogatory sense. Thus, if a tout suggests a winning horse, the player will say, "I got a tip on the winner." But if the horse loses, he will say, "I was *touted* on Lazy Fox."

Touting, since it concerns in some way the making of easy money, is a setup for a con game. In one version, the con man poses as an owner, trainer, jockey, exercise boy, or one having familiar contact with a stable. The con man takes advantage of the easy informality at the track by using such conversation gambits as "Who do you like in the race?" After one of the races, when a long shot wins, the con man appears with two $10 win tickets on the longshot winner. The mark, with whom conversational friendship has already been established, will ask how the con man picked that horse. The "roper" will inform the mark that such horses can't be picked out of the *Form;* what one needs is inside information. He goes on to explain that he gets his tips from his brother, a certain sharp trainer who handles a small string of horses. The roper tells the mark that he has to meet his brother after a certain race because the latter knows a good thing is going. The roper brings the mark along to meet the trainer, who now appears in the full splendor of his role: binoculars around neck, sharply polished riding boots, and a tag on lapel that says "owner-trainer."

Many players believe that the only people who really beat the game are those with inside information. notably the stable help and particularly the trainer. If the con man can successfully impersonate one of these roles, he is in a position to exploit the gullibility of others.

After the usual ploy of can-we-trust-this-guy and sure-he's-a-friend-of-mine, the mark is asked to put up $100—good-will money, "something for the boys." The rest of the story is too well known to belabor.[34]

The more common touting operation is the following: After establishing contacts, sometimes taking several weeks, the tout tells his clients he has something hot going, and will relinquish his information if the clients put down a $20 or $50 bet for him. And when the horse wins he will collect the winning ticket. The tout then finds a race where there are four logical contenders and gives a different horse to four different persons. In about 85 per cent of the cases, one of the four logical contenders will win and one will run in the money. The winners will be elated, and the players who backed the horse that ran in the money will often give the tout a second chance. For any given race, he will get to as many as sixteen persons. That means that about four of them in any race will have a winner and another four will try him again. For the next race, the tout gets different clients and distributes the selections as in the previous case. The reason he doesn't use the same group for consecutive races is that people become suspicious of too much information, but will accept the notion of two hot tips a day.

To keep up with all his clients, the tout sometimes uses differ-

34. For a summary of conning operations see E. H. Sutherland (Ed.), *The Professional Thief* (Chicago: University of Chicago Press, 1937), chapter 3.

ent color chalks to mark them. When players are spotted with chalk marks on their backs, one can be sure that a tout is operating at the track. It is one of the things that the track police are on the lookout for. We will have more to say about touts in the next chapter where we turn our concern to the occasionals.

6.

THE OCCASIONALS

At least four-fifths of the crowd on any given day is made up of "occasionals," individuals who attend the track perhaps several times in a 55-day meet or as infrequently as once a year. Although most players are occasionals, the character of the audience is relatively uniform; for it is *structured* by the social occasion itself. Like other "social occasions," the race track is a temporally and spatially bounded situation where a standard pattern of conduct is recognized as appropriate or official.[1]

One of the most obvious features of horse racing is that it occurs in a social arena that has ecological boundaries. Since no visible external events intrude on the action, the race track constitutes a little cosmos of its own.

Besides these physical boundaries, social action is contained by certain "rules of irrelevance"[2] (that is, persons at the track share an understanding that certain perspectives are to be excluded). Social class and other background characteristics of the players are excluded as relevant in this area. External identities are also irrelevant, and, indeed, a race track norm prohibits inquiring into the background or even names of fellow players. Not only are external identities excluded, but by permitting the player to exercise new skills and rationalities, horse racing generates *new*

1. Goffman, *Behavior in Public Places, op. cit.,* p. 18.
2. For a discussion of rules of irrelevance see Goffman, *Encounters, op. cit.,* p. 19 ff.

113

identities. At the track, Sammy the painter becames Sammy the handicapper.

Moreover, and in part because of the physical and psychological features just mentioned, boundaries are maintained because of the similarity of behavior of the social actors present on the scene. Because the individual at the track is engrossed in an action in the presence of others similarly engrossed, the *reality* of his "field of consciousness" is confirmed and thrust upon him with clearness and distinctness.[3] In other words, the reality experienced is an all-embracing reality. If during the race an observer should glance at the crowd, he would not find many, if any, persons focusing their visual and cognitive attention on other matters. In this respect, an unexpected difference exists between a horse race and a bull fight. The latter may seem to be the epitome of excitement since it involves a matter of life and death. But a bull fight can last ten to twelve minutes, and if it is obvious at some point that the matador is in poor form, attention can flag and boredom becomes visible. While not a matter of life and death, the horse race unfailingly commands absorbed attention.

As in other social occasions, one finds at the track a variety of rituals and customs. For instance, a well-defined system of etiquette guides the behavior of the spectators during the running of the race. For instance, the management of standing and sitting is governed by a system of norms. In a distance race where the horses start in front of the grandstand, the spectators are expected to keep their seats until the horses have swung around the first turn (called the "club house turn") and head into the backstretch. At that time, one may get to one's feet, but standing on one's chair is a violation of etiquette. When, finally, the horses have entered the last turn and straightened out into the homestretch, one may climb on his chair. To stand on one's seat before the horses have entered the stretch would call for informal sanctions such as being

3. For a further clarification of this abstract remark see Aron Gurwitsch, *The Field of Consciousness* (Pittsburgh: Duquesne University Press, 1964), and Maurice Merleau-Ponty, *The Primacy of Perception and Other Essays* (ed. by J. M. Edie; Evanston: Northwestern University Press, 1964).

yelled at or slapped on the shoulder with a program. Thus by observing the audience as they go through the three stages of sitting, standing, and climbing, one can predict where the horses are at any point in the race. When the horses start in the backstretch (as is typically the case in a sprint race), one may stand to watch the start; but again one appropriately waits until the homestretch to climb on the chair. These rules of etiquette are nowhere printed nor are they ever discussed—and yet they are known and practiced as common understandings of what constitutes normal behavior.

Rooting and shouting one's horse home is also governed by rules of etiquette. While a spectator may mildly root for his horse throughout the race, only when the horses have an eighth of a mile to run may he start shouting. If he should scream home his winner *before* that point, he is told to shut up by those around him. On the other hand, if a person is noticeably disinvolved, others standing next to him may attempt to stir his adrenals by a sharp slap on the back.

As in other types of social occasions, the track generates many temporary and diffuse relationships. For instance, strangers entering into conversation may discuss the chances of a certain long shot. The players may have already made their selections and placed their bets; however, if they agree on the long shot, one will suggest to the other that they enter into partnership, put in a dollar apiece and play the horse. Such suggestions are almost always acted upon. One person makes the bet, taking with him the stranger's dollar. If the horse wins, the person making the bet could return after the race and say he was "shut out" (that is, he couldn't get to the window on time); or he could simply disappear in the crowd, keeping both halves of the winning ticket. But this would be a gross violation of the norms of trust that one expects others at the track to share. These norms of trust are reinforced by a sense of camaraderie. Among racegoers, the kinship felt is similar to that experienced in collegial relations to be found when, for instance, two unacquainted professionals meet at a convention. Strangers at the track are eager to share stories of past successes and failures—the time the player won the $1,000 daily double, the time he hit the four-horse parlay, or the time he missed by a nose when $100 was running on a 20-to-1 shot.

Comradeship, however, is an emergent property of the race track and not the primary reason for the game's attraction. Nor would it be correct to say that the primary reason is the opportunity to make money (not at least for the occasional). The great bulk of players do not regard betting the horses as a way of becoming wealthy or even as a profitable pastime. The occasional, in contrast to the regular, does not expect to win but only hopes to.[4] In fact occasionals define success as breaking even. If they should lose—well, that's what recreation costs; and if they should win—well, that's what happiness is.[5]

SOCIOLOGICAL THEORIES ON
THE LURE OF THE TRACK

Sociologists theorizing on the reasons why men gamble have emphasized its tension-management function.[6] Conformity to normative expectations in the occupational sphere—with its emphasis on the pattern-variable profile of universalism, functional specificity, and affective neutrality—runs counter to the impulsive side of man.[7] Gambling, presumably, represents a release for these cumulative tensions. The sociological problem, however, is not only to answer the question of why men gamble, but why the race track should be the preferred arena for gambling for so many. Devereux has suggested a plausible answer: horse racing is not only a mechanism for tension management, but it is a culturally sanctioned form of gambling. In a country with a Puritan bias against all

4. Devereux, who has no conception of the professional gambler as discussed in the previous chapter, mistakenly asserts that all players merely hope to make money (*op. cit.*, p. 698).

5. Compare the observations by Whyte, *op. cit.*, p. 141.

6. Herbert A. Bloch, "The Sociology of Gambling," *American Journal of Sociology*, 57 (1951), pp. 215–222. See also Devereux, *op. cit.*, p. 79, and Talcott Parsons, *The Social System* (New York: Free Press of Glencoe, 1951), p. 308.

7. Parsons, *ibid.*, pp. 180–200.

forms of gambling, race track gambling is a legitimated activity and is consequently a sanctioned outlet to handle tensions. This sanctioned quality of horse race gambling, then, is of particular importance to a Protestant ethic-oriented middle class.

An important qualification should be noted concerning Devereux's position. By accepting the notion of a single normative structure, he overlooks various "subterranean values"—particularly a "sporting ethic"—that have long been part of the American scene.[8] Thus early American race tracks were built near churches so that the fans wouldn't have too far to walk to enjoy their favorite recreation, or to observe the gambling activities of those two well-known regulars, George Washington and Thomas Jefferson. Despite this qualification, Devereux's remarks on horse racing as a sanctioned form of gambling are worth quoting:

> Although horse racing has always been associated with gambling, and although it depends upon gambling money for its principal economic support, and although it draws heavily upon gambling motivations to sustain interest, these gambling elements are somewhat better disguised in horse racing than in most other forms of gambling. Horse racing is also a sport, wholesome enough in its own right, and an industry providing more or less legitimate employment for thousands of persons. In spite of certain doubts and suspicions, deeply rooted in the cultural structure, about the moral worth of horse racing and about the status of the various professional and amateur members of turf society, the sport has always maintained a formal facade of fashion and respectability. And furthermore, horse racing has a socially approved function to perform; to improve the breed of horses and horsemanship.[9]
>
> . . . .
>
> [Thus horse racing] comes neatly tagged with a parcel of ready-made rationalizations. The gambling elements are disguised under a facade of culturally acceptable contexts; the respectable clientele, the decorum and codes of honor, the interests in sporting and in thoroughbred horses, together with such extrinsic elements as going to Saratoga to take the salts, served neatly to conceal the conflict with other basic norms within the same culture.[10]

8. David Matza, "Subterranean Traditions of Youth," *Annals* (November 1961), pp. 102–118.
9. Devereux, *op. cit.*, p. 258.
10. *Ibid.*, p. 261.

Irving Zola, in his study of gambling in a lower-class setting, supplements Devereux's analysis. He agrees with Devereux that financial success is not the primary motive or even essential motive for playing the horses. But while Devereux emphasizes the tension-management function of horse racing, Zola places greater weight on the intrinsic rewards of the activity itself. These rewards involve the exercise of rationality and a sense of control over one's destiny. Thus Zola notes that the man who handicapped his own horses gained more prestige in his group than the man whose selections were based on "hot tips" or the use of "inside information." It is the exercise of rationality and not the access to hot information that demonstrates skill and control over one's destiny.[11]

My own interviews and observations are in accord with Zola's findings. In the following interview, the player—asked why he bet on horses—emphasized the importance of the exercise of rationality:

> Why? I'm a tailor with a nice place and two helpers. So in the afternoons, maybe twice a week, I come to the track and buy a *Racing Form*, and make picks. For forty years I do tailoring and don't have to think about it, you know what I mean. Here I can use my *kopf*.

In response to my question, another player remarked tersely, "At work I'm Sammy the painter; here I'm Sammy the handicapper." Further inquiry indicated that for Sammy, a handicapper meant someone who is using rationality to master a situation. A "storeroom worker" responded along similar lines: "I only went to the eighth-grade, but I'd like to see the college boy that reads them little numbers like me," referring to his ability to make sense of the *Form*. In the following interview the player emphasized why he didn't engage in other forms of gambling:

> It's not like roulette—which I never touch—where you have to beat the house. No one beats the house. And it's not like poker where you sit around and have to look at faces. The only person you have to beat [in horse racing] is your-

11. Zola, *op. cit.,* p. 225.

self. It's all a question of a personal equation [sic], you
have to beat yourself. And if you beat yourself and use
your head you never lose—not too much anyway—you can
enjoy yourself.

In sum, the findings of Devereux and Zola converge with mine.
Taken together, they constitute a challenge to the view that gambling—at least horse race gambling—is a withdrawal or rétreatist
mode of adaptation, or an avenue used by the lower class for a
kind of windfall mobility.[12]

LAY THEORIES ON
BEATING THE GAME

In his efforts to beat the game, the regular's big problem is
that built-in obstacle of horse race gambling, namely, the system
of self-destructive information. Good information, when acted
upon, diminishes its value. While this feature of horse racing also
affects the potential success of the occasional, he—more than the
regular—is additionally hampered by his espousal of certain the-
cries that are adequate only for the practical purpose at hand,
namely, to find a meaningful play.

The essence of many of these lay theories is to take independent events and treat them as dependent. As a general orientation,
the emphasis on the dependence of events is quite reasonable. For
instance, one may reasonably assume that the performance of a
horse in a particular race will be dependent upon his past performances. The problem with the lay theories is that *all* events of
interest to the player are seen as dependent. In those instances
where events are partly dependent, lay theories exaggerate the
dependency.

Such lay theories are of two types. In one type, the idea of
dependence is used to predict the continuance of the same outcome. In a second type, dependence is used to predict a change of

12. This interpretation is suggested by Robert K. Merton, "Social
Structure and Anomie," in *Social Theory and Social Structure* (New York:
Free Press of Glencoe, 1957).

an outcome.[13] An example of a continuance theory is the notion that one should bet a hot jockey. When a jockey is hot, everyone climbs aboard. (As a result, the odds on the horses he rides are considerably lower than they would be if other boys had the same mounts.) An example of a change theory is the notion that if a jockey has won several consecutive races, he is *due* for a loss. (And his next mount will be underplayed.) As we see in the case of jockeys, lay theories tend to come in opposite pairs, and the player is continually switching from theory to theory without a sense of their contradiction.

Another lay theory involves the playing of favorites. Year in and year out, favorites win 30 per cent of all races. Players believe that if a favorite loses a particular race, the chances of one winning the next race increase. Some players back favorites in each race and increase their bet after every loss, because the next one is due. Other players will quote the statistic that the odds are 20 to 1 that on any given day a favorite will win at least one race. If the favorites have lost in the first eight races on any day, these players are likely to bet a bundle on the favorite in the last race on the assumption that the probabilities are now 20 to 1 in their favor.

A popular theory held by players is that "horses owe you money" and that if you extend them credit, they will pay you back. So if a player loses a big bet on a horse, he will continue to bet the animal whenever it runs (regardless of any other betting he does in a particular race). Following this procedure, the player won't be caught, as the race track phrase has it, "looking out of the window" on the day it wins.

Considering that occasionals only hope to win, these theories are adequate for the purposes at hand, namely, to make meaningful decisions. In the following pages, I will discuss still other lay theories.

---

13. For a general discussion see John Cohen and Mark Hansel, *Risk and Gambling* (New York: Philosophical Library, 1956), p. 28 and *passim*.

HANDLING MONEY

In making his bet, the player has a choice of backing a horse to win, place, or show, or any combination thereof. If he wishes to bet his selection win and place, he will have to go to two different windows. If, however, he wishes to back a horse win, place, and show he may go to one window that distributes a "combination ticket" covering such across-the-board betting. At most tracks, one will find a $6 combination window and (less frequently) a $15 combination window, which means, respectively, that the player bets $2 and $5 on the first, second, and third position. Should the player wish to bet $33 across the board, say $15 win, $10 place, and $8 show, he will have to go to three separate windows. Some players bet only win, others only place, still others only show. Most players have no prearranged pattern and will vary the way they play depending on the kind of race, the degree of certainty, and the amount of available capital. Idiosyncratic factors are also at work. For instance, one player explained that his style of betting had changed over the years in accord with the growth of his family. Before he was married he played only to win. After he was married, he played win and place. When their first child arrived, he played across-the-board. With the second child, he played only place. Now that he has three children, he he plays only show. He reports that his losses are even greater now, but he feels less guilty about gambling because betting for show is not really gambling—and a man with family responsibilities shouldn't gamble.

The denominations of the sellers' windows are $2, $5, $10, $50, and, at the very largest tracks, $100. The heaviest betting is done at the $2 window, but this doesn't mean that $2 is the modal bet. Players will purchase two or three (or more) tickets on the same horse at the $2 window, preferring to play $4 or $6 on their selections rather than $5, since the mutuels are calculated in terms of $2 bets—and the fan can figure out the payoffs more easily with $2 mutuel tickets. Thus, $5 windows are unpopular at the track, and are far less numerous than $10 windows. It appears that the major traffic at the $5 windows comes from those people who are discouraged by the long lines at the $2 or $10 windows. On an average, the fan (at the larger tracks) pumps into the machines about $90 in a day of racing, or an average of $10 per race.[14] Not all this is fresh money, but money rebet from winnings.

One of the questions that I have continually posed to players is, "When you've had a winner, do you ever let your money ride?" Players say that they sometimes let the whole thing ride in the last race, after first deducting the sum that would make them even for the day. By this procedure, they say, they cannot lose. If the horse wins, it is all gravy; if not, they are even— which is what they had hoped for in the first place. With the exception of the last-race plunge, players are not wont to let it ride. The following player captured the essence of all the other persons interviewed: "If my horses are winning, I make bigger bets. But to bet everything? You think I'm a *mishugenah?* Who's to impress?"

The remark "Who's to impress?" is particularly relevant to the pattern of betting among players. Most players attend the track alone, and hence their activities are not open to the inspection of others. The casino gambler, on the other hand, is subject to the pressures of an audience that might egg him on to bet in a manner contrary to his own inclinations. The motive of the casino audience is to encourage a display of moral character, demonstrated by "letting it ride."

Even when players attend the track with others, informal arrangements and common understandings dictate that they will not inquire into each other's betting. Sample remark by a player: "When I go with someone, we have a rule. He doesn't tell me and I don't tell him [how much each bets]." Reports another: "Sometimes we chip in together on a horse. Then we bet whatever we want and how much we don't talk about." The absence of an observing audience that stands ready to egg on a player to demonstrate moral character by "letting it ride" is one source of conservative play.

14. For a further discussion of betting action see the precise study by Herman, *op. cit.*

Some evidence that loners (at least) do not "let it ride" is supplied in a quantitative study of race track betting. At one point in his study, Herman interviewed a quota sample of 100 persons from the grandstand and the clubhouse, asking: "When you win, do you usually rebet all of your winnings right away or what . . . ?" Herman reports that 11 per cent rebet all winnings immediately; 3 per cent said they do so eventually; 34 per cent rebet a fixed ratio of the winnings; and 41 per cent answered "No." [15] He interprets these results as indicating that players are essentially conservative in the handling of money, which agrees with my position.

Generally speaking, then, the characteristic of the player is his conservativeness. Two ways of minimizing risk are *covering the bet* and *playing the favorite*. Covering the bet refers to a variety of betting devices that serve the same end: to insure security. One way to minimize risk is to bet a horse across the board; so if the animal should be "photoed out" of the win or place money, the player at least gets something back. Another method is to bet more than one horse in a race, or to bet them in such a way that a loss is cushioned and a win is maximized. Thus the player who bets two horses in a race will place $2 on a 5-to-1 shot and $10 on a 2-to-1 shot. If the 5-to-1 shot wins, he is even; if the 2-to-1 shot wins, he has made a nice profit on the investment. The various methods of covering one's bet have the same aim: to arrange one's betting in such a way that the worst outcome will be breaking even.[16] For the player, breaking even means staying ahead of the game. Although he is no better off than before, he has had the action that might have meant a profit. He has taken a risk and enjoys the reward of having been where the action is.

Covering one's bet is the typical manner of playing *before* success has graced the player. But once the player finds himself cashing winning tickets and is clearly ahead covering the bet gives way to another device of security—eating chalk, that is, betting the favorite. Because the favorite statistically has the best chance

15. *Ibid.*
16. The notion of covering one's bets to at least break even is likely to be characteristic of many interpersonal situations, but this potentially fruitful topic cannot be explored here.

of winning, the player sees this course of action as one way of minimizing risk.

Here, in sum, are some of the generalizations emerging from our investigation of handling money. To begin with, we can say that as the player wins he will increase his bets (though not recklessly "letting it ride") but will select the favorite. Second, the longer the odds, the less he will bet; the shorter the odds, the more he will bet. In addition, when the player is operating on his own rather than the track's money, he will make an effort to cover his bet—and in such a way that he feels will "minimize risk" and "maximize profit." And, finally, reckless betting—when it occurs —will occur more frequently when an audience is present to witness or encourage the player's display of a kind of moral courage.

Now that these empirical generalizations have been stated, a major exception must be noted. This exception involves the last race of the day. Players have endowed the last race with special significance. While no special term is used to designate other races, the last race has a variety of names: the nightcap, the getaway race, the dog race, the jockeys' race. For the player, the last race is his *final* opportunity to break even or make his killing, and thus different rules and behavior patterns emerge. Similarly in poker, the last game is sometimes played under different rules or stakes. And in the same sense, in many pickup bars—and especially in the notorious homosexual ones—the last hour is often one where caution is thrown to the wind, the pace of activity frantic, and, in effect, "long shots" become more likely candidates than they were earlier in the evening.

For a majority of players, the problem they face as they prepare their strategy for the last race is how "to get well," that is, how to get even. To get even, two alternatives are open to the player: he can bet heavily on a favorite, or bet lightly on a long shot. His choice will depend for the most part on his capital. If the player has sufficient capital to make a heavy bet on the favorite, he will choose this course. For instance, if he is behind $100, he will bet $50 on the 2-to-1 favorite. But if he has only $10 left, he will search for a horse that will run at odds of about 10 to 1.

Players who ordinarily stick with either the first, second, or third choice in the betting will suddenly be plunging on outsiders. The man who has all day been rational and conservative is suddenly a reckless mystic looking for miracles. Of course, that is not the way he sees it. Theories have emerged about the last race that permit the player to retain an image as one conducting himself in a rational and disciplined way while stabbing for long shots. One theory holds that the last race is the jockeys' race. And since the jockeys want to get the most for their investment, the player reasons that the horse they will "permit" to win will be an outsider. Thus, in the last race, the decision to play an outsider is reasonable, where the grounds for choosing such a horse in other races would not be. The theory is kept alive by the slim evidence that when anything that might be called a jockeys' race occurs, it does in fact come off in the last race. But for the players who are stabbing for a long shot, *every* last race is a jockeys' race—except when they have the capital to back the favorite.

A second theory about the last race is based on the fact that the cheapest claimers are programmed for this race. The theory holds that in a "dog race" (the cheapest claiming race), one can throw, if not caution, then at least form, to the winds. In this type of race, it is believed, almost anything can happen: The horses entered are supposedly erratic in their performance; therefore one can't take the past performance charts at face value. Of course, the same player, after pronouncing this theory, will turn to the past performance charts to glean signs—taken at face value —that the horse somewhere in his history has shown a glimmer of life. And where the *Form* does not disclose such glimmerings, the player will search elsewhere for signs: the jockey, the breeding, or even the color of the horse. Some jockeys are said to ride better in the last race; some sires are said to produce good route horses (the longer distances are programmed for the last race) ; and grays are said to do well in the last race (because grays run best in the evening and the last race is the closest to nightfall).

MAKING A BET

Nine races typically make up what is called the day's "card." The occasional generally plays in each race. Since there is a thirty-minute wait between races (which will last less than two minutes), he will be making about two decisions an hour. This seems like an inordinately long time to wait for "action," especially compared with the rapid decision-making pressures placed on, say, the casino's blackjack player. But for the race track gambler, the half-hour between races is not "dead" time. After each race, one needs a few minutes to recover from the excitement—of success or failure. A few minutes more are spent in discussing the event with one's conversational partner (often a stranger) or in reexamining the race in the *Form* in an attempt to make sense of the event just witnessed. For the winners, there is the rush to the cashiers for the payoff; for the losers, a trip to one of the many refreshment stands. About five minutes after the race is declared official, a bell rings announcing that the sellers' windows are now open for betting, and once again it is time to mobilize for action. The player, let us say, has one or two possible selections in this race, and a close look at the horses in the paddock may help him make up his mind. No sooner has he arrived at the paddock than he hears the paddock judge call for "riders up," and a moment later the horses step onto the track to the bugler's call. "The horses are on the track," the public address announcer calls out; it is about time the players made their selections and started heading to the betting windows. But our man is walking along the rail, watching how his selections are acting in the post parade. In observing the horses, he is continually sifting bits of information. *Any* divergence from typicality is taken into account and evaluated for its expressive content. If a jockey pats a horse's neck, the player will inquire to determine if this is typical. If a horse defecates during the post parade, the player may be forced to reevaluate his figures, reading in the animal's droppings the trainer's planned betting coup. Now the moment is fast approaching for a decision. A glance at the odds of the horses, a final look at the *Form* and a last-minute evaluation of the horses' probabilities and the posted odds. Suddenly a klaxon blasts a five-minutes-left-before-post-time signal. By the time he has reached the betting window, the track announcer is saying, "The horses are approaching the starting gate." He places his bet and rushes back to his seat. As he focuses his binoculars, the announcer reports, "They're at the post." He finds his selection in his lens and then quickly glances at the tote board for the final flash of odds. "The flag is up," the announcer says, meaning all the horses are in their stalls ready to charge as soon as the starter releases them with a press of the button. "They're off!" And while the last half hour seemed very short, the next minute and ten seconds will seem very long.

Because of the pressures of the cycle of events between races, the player will need to have some idea before the first race as to his possible selections for all the following races. He needs, as it were, some preliminary information. For most players, this means studying the *Racing Form*, and the stands during the hour preceding the first race have the atmosphere of a university study hall. The horses in every race will be divided into four major categories: the "favorite," the "threats," the "factors," and the "outsiders." The favorite is the "solid" horse, the horse with the best form or the one posted in the program as the morning-line favorite. The threats will consist, first of all, of the "dark horse," one who runs in and out, depending on the trainer's intentions, and second, the "class horse," one that does not have recent good form, but in the past raced with better company. Then there are the "factors," horses that don't have much chance of winning, but whose presence in the race can influence the outcome (for instance, a front-running horse that can press the pace). Finally, there are the "outsiders," horses whose past performances show they have little chance of running with the pack. All the above are categories in use, employed by players to make sense of the social world of horse racing.

In making his general evaluations the player can and often does lean on the experts. The experts most frequently relied upon are the selectors (known as "handicappers") of the *Racing Form*, the local newspaper turf analyst, and the handicappers of the scratch sheet. The scratch sheet, so named because morning editions of this four-page publication list the horses declared or "scratched" from the day's entries, does not give any more information about horses than the local newspaper; but some players believe that its handicappers are superior to newspaper selectors.

During one racing season, I made an effort to locate "illiterate" horse players to find out how they arrived at their selections. I managed to locate six persons (one male, a "worker's helper," and five females, three domestics, one waitress, one cook) who could barely read the names of entrants on the program. All admitted to having less than a sixth-grade education. Their technique of selecting horses was a variation of the following method: The player purchases all the local newspapers and clips out the selections of the various handicappers. Using as many as twenty of these expert informants, the player systematically calculates a rank-order distribution of the horses. The horse selected most often by the experts is "the real good horse"; the horse mentioned second most often is the "gotta watch horse"; mentioned third most frequently, the "take-a-chance horse"; mentioned fourth most frequently, "my long-shot pick." (The methodology of "stupid" people is not unlike that of the sociologist who enters a community, locates the expert informants and asks them to rank the power elite.)

Another type of expert that some players rely upon is the tout, who appears in several shapes and sizes. The smallest type of operation consists of a man with a small hand press. He has a list of clients who receive his daily ratings for a small weekly, monthly, or seasonal fee. A rundown is given on each horse in the race along with his selections. As the customer sees it, one of the advantages of such a sheet is that its small circulation will not have much effect on the betting mutuels; whereas the rundown of horses that appears in the *Racing Form* or local newspaper typically has a large following that affects the odds.

Another touting enterprise is the "colored card." For fifty cents or a dollar, the player can purchase the selections of Bob's orange card, Hermit's green card, Tom's blue card, etc. These cards must be licensed as an information-selling agency, and permission must be obtained from the track to set up stands to hawk them. When on any given day the card is successful, picking three or more winners, the hawkers distribute the cards to the patrons as they file out of the track, shouting, "Three more winners today on Bob's! Bob's gives you winners." When the card is unsuccessful, the hawkers are absent. The occasional player who receives an end-of-the-day successful card might get the feeling that such success is routine for Bob or Tom or Hermit, and so try one the next visit. Before track officials supervised the activities of these hawkers, it was a common practice to set up a handpress in a truck near the track and, printing after the results were known, roll off the winners of every race, showing the infallibility of such hot information. The system "worked" since the cards were sold on alternate days. That is, on the days they "picked" the winners of every race, no cards were sold.

The card touts typically make no pretense at possessing inside information. However, another touting operation plays on the notion of inside information—and some of it is the real thing. Two types of touting agencies can be distinguished. The first plays on the illusion that they are supplying inside information. This illusion is sustained in radio and newspaper advertising. These touts sport such names as the Masked Trainer, the Ex-Jockey, Clocker Smith, and so on. These names help sustain the image that the agencies are staffed by ex-horsemen who have inside contacts. In actuality, the operation is one of doping out winners from the *Form* and hoping for the best. Given his selection, the client is asked either to put no money down but to place a bet for the Masked Trainer, or to pay in advance a set fee, anywhere from $10 to $200 depending on the supposed source of information and the type of quota restriction employed. The $200 special, however, can be bargained for—for, say, $40.

The second type of "insider" touting agency does have connections. It never advertises. The agency typically guarantees $1,000 to the trainer (a syndicate man) for a horse that will be trying and has a good chance to win. This information is sold for, say, $5,000 to 25 of the agent's clients for a fee of $200 apiece. Unless the client is given a string of losers, he will typically stick with the agent, who always guarantees—and the result charts of the *Racing Form* bear him out—a "running" horse. His clients are usually persons who simply like to bet either at the track or through a bookie and demand only the certainty that a horse will be out winging for all the money.

Regardless of the source, most players will have upon entering the track a rough idea as to the horses they consider to be the contenders. Their final selection will depend upon probabilities and odds. If the subjective probability of a horse winning is greater than the posted odds, that horse will be the selection. However, if the odds on a horse suddenly plummet, the subjective probability skyrockets. Like Weber's Calvinists, the players are searching for signs of success and the best indicator, they believe, is the action of "smart money." The players' concept of smart money refers to the betting activities of those people who are really in control of things, and they infer the presence of smart money by a sudden drop in odds on a horse. This theory of smart money is the result of organizational ignorance. In fact, when betting stables and their clients heavily back an animal, they feed the machines slowly so no precipitous change in odds occurs. And the heaviest stable play is delayed until the very last minute, so that the fans cannot capitalize on a dramatic shift of odds. Through these methods, insiders control information about "good things."

Except for the theory of "smart money," players are at a loss to account for a horse's precipitous drop in odds, shifting for instance from 10 to 1 to 2 to 1 in the course of one ninety-second cycle of betting. This can occur, so the theory goes, only because of the action of smart money. Horses that become favorites because of the operation of smart money and then lose are termed "false favorites" in the sense that they go off at odds smaller than their objective form as read in the past performance charts would warrant. However, a false favorite can only be distinguished from a "good thing" (in other words, a winning horse that is bet down because of smart-money action) *after* the race. Thus until proven otherwise, the player will assume that the action of smart money points to sure things. Now, aside from the betting stables' action, where does the "smart money" come from, causing a sharp drop in odds?

One place is mechanical failure. The mutuel machines have been known to go haywire and ring up tickets on some horse. Fans read the sudden drop as indicative of smart-money action and rush to get in on the good thing. Because of such malfunctioning and the crowd's response to its observable consequences, a 30-to-1 shot can quickly become an odds-on favorite.

Another source of a sudden drop in odds is the betting activity of free-wheeling speculators, such as movie or TV celebrities.[17] I was present at California's Golden Gate track when the TV star of a medical soap opera played a hunch and bet a huge sum on a horse by the name of "Physician." After the odds on the horse suddenly dropped, the rumor swept through the turf club and clubhouse that the stable was backing a sure thing, which went off as a hot favorite. That the horse won the race merely confirmed the theory of smart money.

A third source of "smart money" is the comeback money dumped into the machines by agents of bookie establishments. Suppose a player with hot information puts $10,000 on a horse with his bookie. The bookie, examining the scratch sheet, notes the horse's probable odds are 10 to 1 and he stands to lose $100,000. How does the bookie cope with this situation? The days of bribing jockeys to pull horses are long past. Rather, the bookie proceeds as follows. He has his agent drop $2,000 in the machines early in the betting and lets the players do the rest by way of the bandwagon effect. In this manner, the bookie can engineer a drop from 10 to 1 to even money. If the horse loses, the bookie has made an $8,000 profit. If the horse wins, the bookie pays out only $8,000, which he may see as a $92,000 saving.

Of course, two can play at this game. Consider then the following procedure of certain betting stables. The trainer finds a race where he is virtually certain his horse will come home a winner. The horse has recently run close up for $5,000, and today

17. On the attraction of horse race gambling for Hollywood celebrities see Leo Rosten, "The Adoration of the Nag," in Robert D. Herman (Ed.), *Gambling, op. cit.*

will be dropped into a soft spot, $3,500 claimer. Of course, the trainer expects that his horse will be installed as a 7 to 5 favorite on the morning line. He then bets $5,000 with the bookie. The bookie, checking the scratch sheet, notes that the horse is the handicappers' best bet of the day; he figures that the horse will go off at even money, and if it wins, it will cost him only $5,000; he can write that off as "good will" money. In short, he relaxes. At the track, meanwhile, the trainer or his beard dumps $1,000 on horse Y, a logical contender. The drop is timed so that the odds will plummet dramatically. As the players stampede to get with the smart money, the trainer's horse goes up in odds and perhaps leaves the gate at 7 to 1. Result: the bookie is out $35,000. The bookie's only counterstrategy is to place at the track what is called a "free agent," who counters the trainer's action with his own betting action. But such countermaneuvers are typically unsuccessful. First, because the trainer has the jump on the agent, once the stampede begins, the agent will have to put so much money in the machines that the bookie will lose regardless of the outcome. A second advantage the trainer has in this game of strategy and counterstrategy is that the bet he places with the bookie may come so close to post time that the bookie may have communication problems getting word back to his agent to stop a betting trend. The big bookie's only effective solution to this problem is to follow the lead of "louse books" (the small, independent bookies) and to screen all players so that bets are accepted only from a steady clientele of racing illiterates.

The final source of "smart money" is the activity of inexperienced players who have come across "inside information." Untutored in the dynamics of crowd psychology, they dump money in the machines too early and in one lump sum.

At the Window

Once the player has made his selection and is prepared to bet he must face "the meanest man at the track"—the ticket seller.

For the player frequenting the $2 selling windows, the watch word is *caveat emptor:* let the player beware. One shady move used on the unsuspecting player is the "slow count." To illustrate the point, if the player bets $2 on a horse and gives the seller $20, the seller may return change in the following manner: he will very slowly count out three $1 bills and with a flourish of finality snap down a $5 bill with a flair that closes the transaction. Frequently, the person will pick up the $8, turn, and walk away—a victim of the slow count.

A newcomer to the track is usually a $2 bettor. While first learning the ropes, he makes small bets, though the denomination of his bets may increase later. Therefore, the $2-seller is confronted with initiating the newcomer into the folkways of betting. Here is what often happens:

A player wishes to place, say, $4 on horse No. 3. The correct way of making this bet would be to tell the seller: "No. 3, two times." Suppose, however, he says: "Two tickets on No. 3." He is most likely to get tickets on the No. 2 horse, since the seller is used to hearing the number of the post position of the horse called first, followed by the number of tickets one wants to purchase. Newcomers often make this mistake leading immediately to disputes. "Why the hell don't you pay attention to what you're doing," the seller will say. "But," the newcomer will reply, meekly or truculently, "I asked for No. 3." The player will often accept the tickets and read the event as a matter of fate—after all that horse could win, and as a newcomer to the scene he probably doesn't have much conviction or reason for supporting his original choice—and may now feel that the mistake on the part of the seller adds some touch of kismet to the already mysterious enterprise of divining winners.

The Daily Double

Barring the last race, players generally exercise restraint and rationality in their betting. But another exception deserves special mention: the daily double.

In the daily double, the player must pick the winner of the

first and second races. Since the daily double is a separate pool, players do not know how the betting is affecting the odds, and a betting stable can put down large chunks of daily-double money without the public becoming aware. Thus the shrewd trainer who wishes to disguise his betting designs will attempt to place "running" horses in both the first and second races and will bet the double.

One of the rational components of race track gambling is the calculation of a horse's probability of winning against the posted odds. But since the odds, as affected by the wagering, are not posted for the daily double, there is a structural arrangement conducive to irrational behavior. In fact, the daily double is something of an institutionalized ritual of irrationality—perhaps one that has a functional role in managing the tensions that accompany the more rational and disciplined efforts of the players in all the other races.[18] Otherwise put, a sanctioned reversal of normal activities may serve to maintain conformity to the normal routines.[19]

The magical and irrational practices associated with other forms of gambling abound in daily-double play. Numerology charts and dream books may be referred to by the otherwise sober player when making daily-double selections. A more popular inspiration is one's age; hence, the player who is 34 years old bets No. 3 in the first race and No. 4 in the second. (When 6 and 5 win the first and second races respectively, the racing news will sometimes note that "the fans on retirement had the daily double today.") Also players will link horses in the double whose names, taken together, have a certain significance. One Negro regular, who ordinarily maintains the strictest care in his selecting and betting, informed me that he always played a double if two horses had names with civil rights implications. On one occasion, I recall, his only two selections for the day—based on an analysis of

18. For a penetrating discussion of ritual role reversal see Max Gluckman, *Custom and Conflict in Africa* (Oxford: Basil Blackwell, 1955), p. 111ff.
19. When, some years back, New York state legislators put an end to the daily double, players went on strike and pressured the state to reverse its ruling, as a functional analyst might have predicted.

past performance records—were running in the first and second race; but rather than play these horses in the daily double (he played his "rational" selections separately), he bet the daily double of two other horses, Equalization and Aid, explaining to me that President Johnson was trying to aid the Negroes through equalization.

Players will also select for their doubles horses with the names of relatives or friends. One regular, whose son is named John, for years "wheeled the book" when the horse Our Son John ran in the first or second race. (He showed no such preference when the horse ran in races other than the double.) To "wheel the book" is to play one horse in one race with all the horses in another race.

Race track regulars with whom I became acquainted always assumed that I had played Scott's Pal, Scott's Choice, or Scott's Blue when these namesakes ran in the daily double. They made no such assumption when the "Scott" horses ran in other races.

In sum, daily double play well illustrates the capacity of individuals to compartmentalize their behavior within the same ecological territory.

7.

PLAYING THE BOOK

Playing with bookies has definite advantages for certain categories of bettors.[1] Some bettors have no choice. Being located in
"track-locked" states, they either play with the books or not at
all. Some players simply prefer the convenience of the bookie. Not
only can one avoid big crowds, but he can continue in his normal
occupational role while indulging in betting. Furthermore, most
books will extend credit, and thus are attractive to some players,
just as shopping with the corner grocer who gives credit is preferred by some to the cash-and-carry supermarkets. Still another
category of player prefers the books because he wants more
action; the track has only a nine-card program. At the books,
however, the player can bet at any track in operation. At the other
extreme is the system player who comes up with about one selection a day and who would rather play with the book than go to
the track and sit out the day for only one race. Finally, certain
professional gamblers prefer the book because their money will
not affect the payoffs, since it will not be placed in the mutuel
machines. Bookie play, in other words, is the only potential
method of overcoming the system of self-destroying information.

Before the advent of parimutuel machines, bookmakers were

1. An estimated two million people bet $8 billion with the books each
year. However, this estimate includes all types of bookmaking—football
pools, prize fights, baseball, etc. Louis A. Lawrence, "Bookmaking,"
Annals, op. cit., p. 46.

free to figure their profit percentage, or "vigorish," [2] by determining the odds that would be offered on the different horses of the race. Thus in a six-horse race if the bookmaker offered odds of 4 to 1 on five of the horses and 9 to 1 on the remaining horse, then no matter which horse won he was assured of a vigorish of 10 per cent.[3] In other words, the bookmaker operated in exactly the same manner as the parimutuel machines operate today.

Today the bookmaker's payoffs are determined by the odds recorded at the tracks—the result of the public play in the mutuel machines. If the bookie play exactly duplicates the parimutuel play, then the vigorish will be identical with the tracks, from 10 to 15 per cent. For the bookies, however, the "take" for each race involves anything from 100 per cent to zero per cent—or, as is often the case, the bookie has a minus pool. Thus while it is theoretically impossible for the track to lose on any race, it is theoretically possible for the bookie to lose on *every* race. The question remains, then, how is it possible for the bookies not only to stay in business but often to achieve greater profits than the track itself?

One answer is for the bookies to organize in such a way that they can duplicate the "track handle" (i.e., the same distribution of play as the track). This assures a profit equivalent to the track take. If the bookie becomes overloaded on any particular horse, he can pass it on to another bookie. This operation, if well organized, guarantees for any one bookie in the organization a profit similar to the track's. But the individual bookie may find two drawbacks. First, he must submit to a centralized control and follow an authority of command whose penalties for violation are said to include murder and other disagreeable sanctions. The second drawback involves the intrinsic limitations of the operation, namely, the mechanical problem of bets flowing in too late to be laid off. Even with organization, the individual bookie can, race

2. While "vigorish" is a term in use by bookies, it is not peculiar to the racing scene but refers to any percentage earned in illegal dealings.

3. As I explained in my discussion of the operation of the dutcher. five horses at 4 to 1 and one at 9 to 1 produce a percentage book of 110 per cent. The percentage over 100 constitutes the track "take" or the bookie's "vigorish."

after race, show a minus pool. And while the bookie can borrow money from the organization to cover all bets and weather slumps, this only places him in deeper debt to centralized domination.

Another answer guarantees success and a margin of profit far above that of the track take. In fact, it might be stated categorically that the long-run success of a bookie depends on it: developing a clientele of "racing illiterates," individuals with an established history of low achievement in handicapping or having limited access to hot information. The motto of the bookie, as described to me by one operator is "dumb play is sure play," meaning that the bookie stays in business so long as he can cultivate the "dumb play."

Restricting one's clientele to dumb play assures fantastic profits, a fact summarized in the statement by one recognized authority:

> An indication of the profits expected by the book may be adduced from the percentage the book is willing to expend in order to get business. Apart from whatever sums are to be used for the buying of protection from the local law enforcement agencies, any book is ready to give up 50 per cent of the profits to his agents for procuring business. Each agent's total monthly returns are tabulated, and 50 per cent of the net losses of the customers dealing directly with him provides his compensation. (In the unlikely event that any particular month shows a net loss to the book, the account is carried over to the next month.) Once the agent has contacted a prospective bettor and furnished him with the telephone number of the book, the customer merely calls the book and places his bet, mentioning the name of the agent who is to receive credit for the transaction.[4]

The value of the bookie's agent is measured by his ability not only to bring in new play, but his ability to solicit dumb play. The bookie's best defense against losses, then, is refusal to accept bets from sharp play.

But even potential sharp play is hamstrung by the structural arrangement whereby the players lack information as to the track odds of the horse. Because track odds are not available to the

4. Lawrence, op. cit., pp. 50–51.

player, he cannot estimate if his subjective evaluation of the horse's chances is greater or less than the posted odds. As pointed out earlier, this calculation of probabilities and odds is at the heart of what may be called rational decision-making. I also noted that when such calculations are impossible because of the absence of posted odds—as in the case, for instance, of daily doubles— the players relax their usual vigilance in handling money. The exact relation between the absence of posted odds and undisciplined play is not clearly understood. However, bookies recognize this relation and even when changing track odds are available to the bookie—as is frequently the case of horse rooms that subscribe to "wire" services—this information is *deliberately* withheld. By trial and error, horse room operators have learned that their profits increase when tracks odds are withheld. We will shortly come back to this relation between the absence of information about track odds and the resulting undisciplined play that serves the interests of the bookie.

In our discussion so far we have been suggesting that, along with certain similarities, different types of bookies have different modes of operation. We will now specify three types of bookies: the louse (or flea) book, the organized book, and the horse room (or bookie joint).

THE LOUSE BOOK

The louse book is a one-man operation. The pattern of relations that typify the louse book and his clients is hard to understand without mentioning the historical background that underlies this relationship. In 1909, New York Governor Charles Evans Hughes pushed through the state legislature a law forbidding race track gambling. This act, in effect, put an end to horse racing in New York, and many tracks closed their doors. Without betting, most spectators lost interest in the sport. But in 1913, to save horse racing from extinction, a modification of the law permitted bookmaking, but ruled that *no money was to be exchanged*. With this ruling, a new form of betting appeared that lasted for nearly

thirty years: a system of "oral betting." Under this system, the
player established credit with the book, and each paid his losses
by check at the end of the day, week, or month.[5] At this time, the
bookie established himself as a man of honor, trust, and fair play.
One student of horse racing summarized the bookie-client relation of those days:

> The bookmakers prided themselves on their honor; and it
> must be said that during this period, which lasted into the
> 1930s, welshing (refusing to pay a gambling debt) was
> almost the exclusive prerogative of the bettor.[6]

Another student writes:

> When the books were operating under the "oral" system of
> betting at the New York tracks, one of the larger book-
> makers had outstanding slightly over $100,000 at the end
> of the season. Asked what he was going to do about it,
> he said, "Try to collect what little I can. Call off the rest,
> and let them start again with me next season. If I don't,
> they will simply bet with someone else, and I might as
> well get what I can before they go overboard again." [7]

The pattern of bookie-client relations established between 1910
and 1940 continues today between the louse book and his clients.
These relations sometimes last a lifetime and are marked by a
sense of mutual trust. Consider the following interview, which I
have found typical of the player's relation with the louse book:

> I've been with the same bookie now for eighteen years. I
> have gone through two wives, but I have never broken up
> with my bookie . . . When you win, he pays immediately,
> he's never welshed on a bet, never gives excuses for not
> paying off right away. And when you're losing he under-
> stands. He never rushes you [to pay off losses]. You know.
> He realizes that you have good periods and bad periods. . . .
> You won't believe this, but he's the only person I trust. I
> mean, I trust him more than my business partner.

5. Parmer, *op. cit.,* p. 169 ff.
6. *Ibid.,* p. 171.
7. Lawrence, *op. cit.,* pp. 51–52.

The subject owns a liquor store and explained that frequently customers ask him where they can locate a bookie. "Many times I asked my bookie if he wants more customers," he said. "I can supply him with plenty through the store, I tell him. But he tells me he doesn't want any more. He says he's not looking for more business but just wants to deal with the people he knows and gets along with." Of course, bookies get along best with steady losers.

Players betting with the louse book admit being steady losers but do not see their relation with the book as an exploitative one, and some express their gratitude, noting that their bookie cancels outstanding debts every year as a Christmas present; where there are no debts he sends them presents ranging from electric shavers to television sets. Above all the bookie is, as his clients report, an "honest guy."

In referring to the integrity of the bookie, I am not suggesting that honesty is an attribute of his character. Rather, honesty is a construct attributed to him by his clientele. Social actors typically come to expect honesty from formal organizations but not from individuals as individuals with whom they enter into a money relation. Hence, we expect honesty from banks, but not necessarily from bankers. The bookie is something of an occupational specialist in managing the impression of honesty. And his task is simplified because players find any display of honesty—by individuals acting as individuals—as amazing.[8] Therefore, players believe that the bookie watches over his customers so they won't go too deeply in debt. They believe further that when a player is in a worse-than-usual slump, the bookie will be hoping along with the player that his next bet wins.

The bookie actively cultivates this trust relationship because he has no sanction of force to ensure that players will pay their debts. The player must view payment as a matter of honor. To help cultivate this trust relationship, the rule is "the customer is always right." Suppose the player phones the book to bet on Big Red in the sixth race, but a Big Rod is running in the sixth and

8. Here, as elsewhere, I am indebted to Goffman, who also informs me that pit bosses in Nevada casinos often turn to their bookies as temporary replacements, since their bookies are the only persons they trust with money.

Big Red is in the seventh. Suppose Big Rod wins and Big Red loses. If the player later contends that Big Rod was his selection and not Big Red, the book will always give him the benefit of the doubt.

In sum, then, the louse book personalizes betting: He is understanding and sympathetic when the player loses; he is an admiring witness when the player has a successful run; and he is trusting like a brother.[9]

THE ORGANIZED BOOK

The predominant form of bookmaking is the "organized book," a loose or well-integrated organization of books operating in a hierarchical arrangement, permitting one book to lay off bets with the larger book above it. Bets are made by phone to an impersonal agent, with a collector or runner dropping by on a daily or weekly basis to pay off or collect from the customers. The larger operators maintain a battery of telephones and take layoffs from the smaller operators as well as handling the action of big bettors. Players who fail to pay off their debts—when dealing with the organized book—may, upon turning the corner some evening, be greeted in the eye by a pair of brass knuckles.

In organization there is strength, and the advantages of organization are many. The smaller operators welded in an organization can operate on the basis of a fixed vigorish, being able to lay off money that overloads the book. By holding bets that are in accord with the bookmaker's percentage table, they are assured a sure profit no matter who wins. The larger operators have the capital, not only to sustain temporary losses, but they can afford to keep

9. A player remarks: "When I have personal problems I don't go to my minister, I go to my bookie. The minister listens, like a bartender. But my bookie helps." Sociologically considered, a bookie is someone to whom a person turns in times of trouble and who extends certain kinds of social credit. A person's bookie may be a wife, a psychiatrist, or a close friend. One might speculate that potential suicides are people without bookies. On the relation between suicide and the absence of someone to turn to, see Harvey Sacks, "The Search for Help" (Unpublished doctoral dissertation, University of California, Berkeley, 1966).

a man stationed at the track who, via walkie-talkie, can be instructed to put down comeback money and perhaps manipulate the track odds as a counter to the activities of the professional gambler operating with the book.

In contrast to the louse book, play with the organized book is impersonal. And players bet not only to win, but to "get back" at the bookie. Touts and system peddlers are familiar with this motivation and advertise their wares as ways to: "Put your bookie out of business," "Knock your bookie for a loop," "Kill your bookie." [10] The evil nature some players attribute to bookies involves the imputed character of the organized members of the species.

THE HORSE ROOM

The horse room, race book, or bookie joint is an off-track gambling *establishment* where horse players may bet. The horse room has been aptly described as a "racket in a goldfish bowl." Unlike the other types of bookmaking, the horse room is a quasi-public place where all comers are welcome (though bets may be refused, that is, the establishment doesn't want the action of some players). Obviously, then, horse rooms cannot operate unless a political "fix" has been arranged. Whenever the police crack down or an anti-gambling reform administration takes office, the horse books are often the first and most obvious targets, since their operation and location is common knowledge in a community.[11]

The player will find listed on the walls in the horse room all the races of the major tracks in operation. Each race appears on a three- to five-foot high white cardboard with black lettering. (The horse room hires a fulltime sign painter for this.) Before each horse's name is a number (not the horse's post position or track program number) that the player uses to indicate his

10. Devereux, *op. cit.*, p. 438.
11. Lawrence, *op. cit.*, p. 49. See also Fred J. Cook, "Racket in a Goldfish Bowl," *The Nation*, 191 (Oct. 22, 1960), pp. 265–272.

selection. The morning line is indicated for each horse. I have observed in recent years that the player is given no further information on the horses' odds, and so he is in the same fix as the track daily-double player, betting without being able to evaluate the horses' chances in terms of its odds. For making rational calculations, the morning line is considered unreliable. Most players soon learn that the morning line bears scant resemblance to the final (or posted) odds. Thus, to be given information on only the morning line is to leave the player virtually bereft of a base line from which to calculate positive expected value. His incapacity to calculate positive expected value —the result of imperfect information—leads the player to relax his normal vigilance in handling money.

In general, then, betting with a bookie structurally deprives the player of just the kind of information he needs to pursue a successful course.

III
the
stage
managers

8.

THE OFFICIAL FAMILY

The official family—the track owners, racing officials, and the state regulatory authorities—constitute the mediating community between the performers and the audience in the racing game. Since I have described various members of the official family earlier, I will be relatively brief in this chapter.

The racing plant is an organization operated by businessmen concerned with turning a profit. If a person (or syndicate) can raise several million dollars, he can fulfill the first requirement in becoming a track owner. But the state will determine if races can be run, when they can be run, and how much profit (or "take") the track can make. By state law, a track is permitted to deduct a percentage from all money wagered in each race. In addition, the track pockets the "breakage" (that is, the odd pennies down to the nearest dime [or nickel] in the payoff prices). For instance, where the exact payoff is $5.87, the player gets back $5.80 and the remaining seven cents is pocketed by the track as breakage. The take and breakage are divided between the state and the track, the specific amount varies from state to state.

The track's take is not all profit. The track must pay for the overhead: the upkeep of the grounds, the payment of track personnel (for example, maintenance men, mutuel men, track of-

ficials, a private police force), and, most important, the purses.
On the average, for each dollar bet 87 per cent goes back to
the players, 6 per cent to the state, 5 per cent to the track, and
2 per cent to the horsemen.[1]

OFFICIAL BODIES

Once the owners have state approval to build a racing plant
and are given certain specified racing dates, the owners declare
themselves a racing association. In 1942 the major associations
in the United States and Canada banded together to form a self-
regulating body known as the Thoroughbred Racing Associations
(TRA). Through this organization, the member tracks attempt
to coordinate and unify the sport. Even those tracks that are
not members are influenced by this, perhaps the most powerful
organization in racing. The major function of the TRA is to
maintain a code of race track standards, including rules regarding bookmaking, wire services, touting, fingerprinting, tattooing,
and identification of horses. The investigative arm of the TRA is
the Thoroughbred Racing Protective Bureau (TRPB). This organization is heavily staffed by former FBI and military counterintelligence agents. Every tip, charge, or rumor of crooked activity is investigated by these men, racing's version of Eliot Ness's
"Untouchables." The waiter serving drinks at the clubhouse bar,
the hot walker in the next barn, the man behind the seller's cage
—any one of these may be a TRPB agent. When these agents are
not on a specific case, they are keeping an eye out for so-called
"blue-cover rogues"—known fixers, crooked gamblers, and touts.
A file is kept on all such violators of racing rules in what is
known as "blue-cover" reports. The rogues in these reports are
barred from all TRA tracks.[2]

Besides keeping lip-tattooed photographs of more than 111,000
horses to aid in identifying the animals, the TRPB also maintains

1. Blanche, *op. cit.*, p. 68.
2. *Inside TRA and TRPB* (New York: Thoroughbred Racing Association, n.d.), p. 39.

a file of some 160,000 sets of fingerprints on all persons in any way connected with racing—racing officials, owners, trainers, jockeys, exercise boys, grooms, etc. Detailed background information is kept on file for more than 25,000 individuals. Given that more than 150 of these undercover agents have 4,300 people under their supervision, it is hard to accept a cultural stereotype that racing is a sport operated by a nationwide Mafia.[3]

Horse racing is a partnership between business and government. The governmental counterpart of the racing association is the state racing commission. Appointed by the governor, the state racing commission "grants the franchise for race track operation, dictates the number of tracks that may operate, limits the number of days of racing, approves purse schedules, passes on the appointment of officials, and licenses jockeys, trainers, and, in some cases, the owners as well."[4] The state racing commission works closely with the TRA, and as a result of the influence of the latter, the state requires—before granting a franchise—that a racing association abide by the racing laws set down by the Jockey Club (to be discussed shortly); these laws have been incorporated in the code of standards of the TRA. The failure of any association to comply with the laws of racing may result in the suspension of an association franchise.

Because horse racing operates under the sanction of the state, the public, in principle, controls racing. If a scandal is uncovered at the track, the public can show its disapproval not only by holding back its support by a dwindling attendance, but by calling for changes through normal political channels. When a new administration is elected in a state, new state racing commissioners frequently are appointed, and these men may take office with a reforming spirit that may be in the interests of the players, the track owners, or the state.

In 1934, the various state racing commissions banded together to form the National Association of State Racing Commissioners (NASRC).

3. *Ibid.*, p. 27.
4. John I. Day, "Horse Racing and the Pari-mutuel," *Annals, op. cit.*, p. 58.

This group has from the outset sought unified action on various racing problems, but inasmuch as any step taken needs individual legislative action in each state, the effect of the NASRC as a national policy-making group has been more influential than actual. It does serve a very useful purpose, however, in bringing racing problems to the attention of the commissioner in each state, and reciprocal action on many rulings is thus brought about.[5]

The idea of reciprocal action is best illustrated in the meting out of sanctions to offenders of the rules of racing. The NASRC has made explicit the common understanding that has always prevailed on the turf: rulings on any track against offenders should be recognized on all tracks. Thus, if a jockey is set down for a foul or if a trainer is "ruled off" a track, these sanctions hold up for all tracks.

The Jockey Club, American racing's oldest regulatory body, serves very much like England's House of Lords: it is mostly an honored and respected institution that has relinquished administrative and regulative functions to other governing bodies, such as the TRA and NASRC. However, since its establishment in 1894, the Jockey Club has maintained two important functions: the approving of all names of horses, and the custodianship of the American Stud Book in which every thoroughbred is registered. A horse may not run on an American track unless it is registered in the Stud Book, thus validating its right to be called a thoroughbred.

TRACK PERSONNEL

To carry out the rules of racing, a track employs a core of personnel with well-defined responsibilities. This official family consists of the stewards, the racing secretary, the paddock judge, the starter, the patrol judges, the placing judges, and the track veterinarians.

---

5. *Ibid.*

Stewards

The stewards are the supreme authority of a race meeting. Typically, each meet has three stewards—one representing the racing association conducting the meeting, one representing the state racing commission, and one representing the Jockey Club, or alternatively, someone appointed by the other two stewards. This elite corps has unannounced access to any part of the grounds or buildings at the plant. Its members can scratch any horse for any reason they see fit. Their powers include ruling on any infraction, demanding proof of the identity of a horse at any time, denying certain horses from running, and conducting investigations of any nature for any reason. Duties of the stewards include resolving terms of disagreement of contracts, adjudicating conflicts about claims, and suspending jockeys, trainers, etc., for misconduct. Besides these duties, the stewards keep a watchful eye on the performances of the horses. If a hot favorite runs out of the money or if a rank outsider suddenly pops home a winner, the stewards may conduct an inquiry, calling the trainer before them to give an account of the sudden turn of fortune. While only the winning horse in a race is given a saliva and urine test, the stewards may call for such tests for any horse, if they have reason to suspect chicanery.

The Racing Secretary

The racing secretary writes the script that determines who the performers will be. In short, the meeting revolves around his work. His first and most important task is to set forth the conditions that will govern the running of all races. About every two weeks, a new "conditions book" appears that states the eligibility requirements for a horse in a given race and the weight he will carry. The conditions are written to suit the available talent and to bring out fields of well-matched horses. There are exceptions to this, however. If many long shots are winning and the percentage of favorites drops substantially below the 30 per cent mark, he will write conditions that will permit one or two standouts to get into a soft field; on the other hand, if the favorites are sweeping the card, the next conditions book will be filled with races that will ensure an open field. In short, the track secretary evaluates what the public wants, and writes a script that will give it to them.

While attending to the public's wishes, the secretary must also keep in mind the wishes of the horsemen. Many horsemen complain that some secretaries are too concerned with the public and do not schedule enough races that will permit all their horses to run—or to run in races where they will have an advantage or favorable opportunity. The racing secretary must always make at least a show of attending to these complaints; for often he must call upon the horsemen to do him certain favors. This is particularly true in the early part of the meet—especially if bad weather has produced an off track—when the secretary will have difficulty filling up the card. He may personally, or through his assistants, encourage horsemen to enter their chargers just for the sake of another entry. This is an institutionalized evasion of the code of racing, but without this patterned deviation, there may be times when no horses are entered for a race. Sometimes if a race does not have enough entries, he will schedule a substitute race or an overnight handicap and send his messengers out to certain trainers to inform them of the race and to encourage them to enter their animals. Despite their continual complaining about the secretary, horsemen will often go far out of their way to help the racing secretary short of entries.

The secretary knows he can command the cooperation of those trainers who wish to get in his good graces because of his second major function—to assign weights in handicap races. Operating in this capacity, the racing secretary is known as the "track handicapper." In adjusting weights for the horses in such a race, the track handicapper is ostensibly concerned with assigning weights in such proportions so that theoretically all horses will cross the finish line at the same time. In general, then, the skill of the track handicapper and the prestige accorded him is measured by the number of close finishes in handicap races. Through common understandings, the trainers enter into a tacit agreement not to let their horses win by too much. A horse that wins a handicap race easily makes the track handicapper look bad. To violate this understanding is a betrayal of trust and is met with harsh sanctions: The next time the horse runs, he is loaded with so much weight that any chance of winning is precluded.

The track handicapper also is subjected to two conflicting pressures from the track owners. On the one hand, the owners want the handicapper to assign weights so that no horse will stand out as a sure thing. The track's owners fear that a standout will lead to a minus pool (which, when it occurs, almost always involves a handicap race, for the bridge jumpers take for granted that in this kind of race the stable is shooting and, in addition, handicap horses are the most reliable performers—they have heart). On the other hand, the track does not want any of the locals stars so overweighted that the trainer will scratch the horse rather than have him "carry a freight train," as the expression goes. Whatever course of action taken by the handicapper, dissatisfaction will usually be felt by either the track owners, the trainer of the "star" horse, or the other trainers in the handicap race.

Given this structural condition of strain, the handicapper will usually cope with the situation by relying on his professionalism and expert knowledge. He relies on formulas that are recognized as legitimate by all parties. For instance, he will use as a universal rule of thumb that one length equals five pounds. Therefore, the trainer of a horse that wins by two lengths can legitimately expect his animal to carry ten pounds more in its next race. Thus, a wise trainer always instructs his jockey to try to win by as close a margin as possible. In this manner, the trainer's instructions to protect his interest has the consequence of protecting the interests of the track handicapper.

The racing secretary is in charge of all stabling accommodations, accepts the horsemen's entries for all the races, and distributes purse money. To perform these duties, the track secretary has a staff—entry clerks, stabling clerks, and so forth.

The Paddock Judge

The paddock judge supervises the saddling of horses in the paddock. Horses that are expected to start in a race must report in the paddock about twenty minutes before post time. If a horse does not arrive on time, the owner and trainer are subject to penalties. The major duty of the paddock judge is to identify the horses as they enter the paddock. He must "know" horses so that a trainer will be unable to slip in a ringer. If the paddock judge has any doubt about the identification of a horse, he reports the matter to the stewards. Immediately, an investigation takes place. The track maintains an identification department where a folder is kept on each horse stabled at the track. In the folder, one finds a full-face and profile photograph of each horse, as well as information on the horse's weight, measurements, and markings. The reason that horses must report to the paddock twenty minutes before post time is to enable the stewards to conduct this inquiry over identification should the paddock judge call for it.

The Starter

The starter is the only member of the official family who has a performer's role. After the horses have completed their parade to the post and have entered the starting gate stalls, the eyes of the audience are focused on the starter. He is responsible for getting all the horses off to a good start. A horse that is caught flatfooted at the start generally has no chance. And unless all the horses break well, the starter is often held to blame. The starter attempts to get all the horses in his field of vision to see that they are in position before springing open the stalls with the press of a button. In order for the starter to have a good performance, the jockeys must cooperate by shouting "Not yet, sir; no chance, sir! No chance!" if for any reason their mounts are not ready. From the time all the horses have been loaded in the gate to the start of the race is generally less than twenty seconds. The gate will open before being released by the starter if forty pounds of pressure are placed on the stall doors. At some tracks, the jockey in post position No. 1 (closest to the starter) has an advantage; for a click sounds from the starter's station in the split-second between the time the button is pressed and the gates open. The jockey that hears this (usually the jockey in post position No. 1) can "jump the bell," and if he has a front running horse, this is a decided advantage. After the starter has released the gate, he pushes a second button that locks the totalizator machines. The interval is about six seconds, long enough for the bellringer to ply his trade.

Patrol Judges

From the time the horses leave the starting gate to the time the last horse passes the finish line, they remain under the close scrutiny of (usually) four patrol judges. Stationed at various points around the track, they watch for fouls, unfair tactics, or jockeys pulling horses. Violations of rules that might lead to the disqualification of a horse are immediately telephoned from their observation towers or from the vehicle that picks them up after each race. When an inquiry is demanded, the jockeys involved are ordered to report immediately to the stewards' room. There, the jockeys, patrol judges, and stewards view the film of the race. By the time the jockeys and patrol judges have reached the stewards' room, the films have been picked up from the several motion picture-equipped towers and processed, ready for showing. As a way of accentuating the honesty and fairness of the stewards' decision, the films are simultaneously shown in the press room. (On rare occasions the press—speaking on behalf of the public—will, after viewing the film, disagree with the official decision.) From the time the patrol judges call for an inquiry to the time a decision has been made takes four to seven minutes. In the interim, the public is informed: The word "inquiry" lights up on the infield tote board, and the track announcer reports the jockeys and horses involved in the inquiry. Even when the patrol judges do not find anything serious enough to call for an on-the-spot investigation, they will report to the stewards anything in the race that was out of the ordinary, such as an unenthusiastic ride by a usually hustling jockey.

Placing Judges

Stationed in a pagoda at the finish line are the three placing judges, who call the finishing positions of the first four animals to cross the finish line. In writing down the finish of the first four horses, the judges operate independently. When they have all done this, they compare notes. If they disagree, they call for a photo. Even if they are in agreement, they will call for a photo if the finish is reasonably close. The word "photo" is flashed on the infield board, and the announcer will indicate which numbers are involved in the photo. After the numbers for the first three positions appear on the tote board, the announcer will remind the players not to destroy their parimutuel tickets until the race is declared official. Before the race is declared official, all the jockeys must return to the area before the pagoda and salute the judges, by raising their hand and thus getting permission to dismount. (Any rider who fails to salute the judges is fined.) After dismounting, the jocks weigh in at the finish line with the clerk of scales, who makes sure that no more than two pounds were lost in the running of the race (this would be automatic ground for disqualification). When the all-clear is given by the clerk of scales and if no objection has been raised by either the patrol judges or jockeys, the race is declared official.

The Vets

The veterinarian is a familiar figure around the track, some big stables employing one or two who devote full attention to their animals and who are paid by the year. Aside from these, at least two veterinarians carry the official title of "track veterinarian," one representing the racing association and another representing the state racing commissioner. At the suggestion of the stewards, the track veterinarian may investigate the condition of any horse stabled on the grounds and pass upon the physical fitness of any animal when some question of its ability to perform is in doubt. Horses that do not pass the inspecting eye of the vet are placed on a publicly posted "vet's list" and are not permitted to enter a subsequent race. The track vets also inspect each horse in a "receiving barn," where the horses stand before being taken to the paddock for saddling. If the vet finds any disability or any evidence of medication, the horse is scratched. According to the rules of racing, no medication can be given a horse within 48 hours before he is to race.

The vets also give saliva tests to every animal that wins a race. In addition, a urinanalysis is given to the winner on a spot-check basis at most tracks. These tests are designed to reveal the use of stimulants that might affect a horse's performance. Spot checks are also made for hypodermic needles and narcotics —the possession of these being forbidden. Thus the barn area is not a "free territory," but is continually subjected to the suspicious eye of the veterinarians and other officials.

9.

CONCLUSION

In discussing information in an interactional framework, I have found it useful to employ a game-type model. To study any sustained interaction as a game, it is not necessary for the participants themselves to conceive of their situation as a game. Rather, to regard any two participants—say, John and Marsha (one might just as easily substitute the United States and the Soviet Union)—as involved in a game they need only fulfill this condition: John, in seeking to realize his goals, takes into account Marsha's expectations of him and also Marsha's expectations of what he expects from her, and vice versa. Since it is hard to conceive of any sustained interaction that does not fulfill this condition, the game framework seems applicable to the study of all social encounters.

Not surprisingly, the "game" concept recently has become a stylish way of referring to a variety of types of relationships, such as sex games, doctor-patient games, husband-wife games, and so on. Instead of an unending list of games, however, theoretical considerations suggest that a more fruitful course is to construct a conceptual framework of formal game models applicable to a wide range of different structures. Specifically, a game framework should involve a generic classification of fundamental forms of interaction, based on the actors' ends-in-view. To illustrate what I have in mind, consider this tentative list of four fundamental forms of interaction conceived in game-model terms: face games, relationship games, exploitation games, and information games.

In *face games*, each participant maneuvers to maximize his own realization of a valued identity, while seeking an equilibrium that will permit others to do likewise.[1] In *relationship games*, the participants seek to create, maintain, attenuate, or terminate personal relations.[2] In *exploitation games*, the participants seek to maximize their position of power and influence vis-à-vis one another. In *information games*, the participants seek to conceal and uncover certain kinds of knowledge.

For any concrete situation, these games are functionally interdependent, empirically overlapping, but analytically distinct. In other words, one may study any sustained encounter (for example, between husband and wife, doctor and patient, host and guest) in terms of these four games at play; these games provide a framework for producing an organized account of stable social action.

But all this is a promissory note. The theoretical task of specifying the types of moves open to the players in each of these games (or some similar classification dealing with fundamental modes of interaction) has scarcely begun. And the following remarks, restricted to only one generic type of game—the information game—are to be regarded as very tentative.

Drawing on our study of horse racing, the task here is to suggest—following very closely formulations by Erving Goffman—the major types of moves involved in *any* information game. To keep the analysis uncomplicated, the information game will be discussed in terms of two players, the trainer and the "seeker." Under the term "seeker," I include other horsemen, members of the audience, and the stage managers (that is, the official family).

The defining features of an information game involve the general types of moves open to the players. The general types of moves in the information game are *recording* moves, *control* moves, *uncovering* moves, and *re-covering* moves.[3]

1. Much rich material on face games can be found in Goffman's essay "On Face Work," *Psychiatry*, 18 (August 1955), pp. 213–231.
2. The concept of "relationship games" and the definition presented here is taken from Goffman's "Strategic Interaction and Communication," *op. cit.*
3. Again, I am indebted to Goffman for the use of these concepts.

RECORDING MOVES

Recording moves refer to the preliminary aspects of the information game. Here the problem involves the kind of information the seeker wants to collect concerning the trainer, including *secret moves, operational code, resolve, information state,* and *resources.*

To begin with, the seeker will want to know about the trainer's *secret moves,* which may be completed, intentioned or initiated. Secret moves, as suggested, may be completed ones. For example, the trainer may have tipped a betting syndicate that he is about to unleash a sleeper, or he may have placed bets with bookies throughout the country. Knowledge about these moves is a strategic piece of information, and the bettor interested in backing a good thing, or a horseman out to claim a sharp animal will profit by knowing about them. If the trainer has decided to put over a sleeper but has not initiated his course of action, one can appropriately describe this state of affairs as an intentioned move. If the trainer has begun to commit his resources to a course of action, as when he secretly works out a horse before a race, we can speak of his activity as an initiated move.

Besides the trainer's secret moves, the seeker will want to know about his *operational code* (that is, the general orientation that influences the way the trainer plays the game). The seeker will attend to three aspects of the trainer's operational code: "preference patterns," "normative constraints," and "styles of play."

To crack the trainer's operational code, then, the seeker will attend—first of all—to the trainer's *preference pattern* (that is, his ordering of goals). Some trainers will prefer to drop a horse down in class to win a bet even though this move increases the likelihood that the animal will be lost via the claiming box; other trainers will prefer to protect the horse from a claim even if it means losing the chance for a betting spot. On a more general level, some trainers prefer to win many races with a horse at short odds, while others prefer few wins with a horse at long odds.

A second component of the trainer's operational code that the seeker will be advised to attend to is *normative constraints*. For instance, moral obligations to the owner prevent most trainers from dropping down a $9,000 horse in a $6,500 claiming race, where the horse can win a sure purse (of which the trainer gets 10 per cent) and the trainer can cash a cinch bet. Also self-imposed restraints will often be sufficient to prevent a trainer from running a sore-legged animal if he believes this will increase its physical suffering.

In following a self-established *style of play*, some trainers, for instance, will shoot only when dropping a horse down in class; some will manipulate a horse only in allowance races, running their animals "honest" in claiming affairs—or vice versa.

To evaluate effectively the secret moves and operational code of the trainer, the seeker will want to know something about the former's *resolve* (that is, the trainer's determination to proceed with the game whatever the costs). Some stables employ clockers to report on fast-working horses that might make good claims. A trainer may learn that such a clocker has spotted his fast-working 2-year-old, which was pointed toward an easy victory in a claiming race. Some trainers will continue with the planned action even when they know their reputation will be hurt when another stable claims their horse and wins with it at higher claiming prices.

Another thing the seeker will want to know about the trainer is his *information state*. For example, the seeker—who might be another trainer—will want to know if his opponent knows about the condition of his own chargers. Or, to complicate the analysis somewhat with another example, the opposing horseman (that is, the seeker) will want to know if the trainer knows that the seeker knows that, say, the trainer typically runs a horse stiff after a layoff before shooting. For if the trainer knows the seeker knows, he will shoot first time out. Of course, and now the analysis becomes truly complicated, the trainer who knows the seeker knows his typical action must assess the possibility that the seeker will anticipate a new action making the change from the typical nonadvantageous to the trainer. The process of mutual assessment can thus be pushed to a point where both parties are left befuddled—but let it stand. The point is that the information state of the trainer is something about which the seeker is advised to collect information.

Finally, the seeker will want to know about the trainer's *resources*. Does he have betting connections? Is his barn overloaded with animals and thus can he afford to drop in claiming price a good horse? Does he have a beard to place bets? Does he work for owners who don't ask questions, leaving the trainer free to wheel and deal with impunity? In addition, the seeker will want to know about his personal attributes. Is the trainer a game-worthy opponent? If not, the seeker will have an advantage, otherwise mutual assessments might lead to the type of befuddlement already mentioned. The seeker will also want to know if the agents who are "playing" for the trainer (for example, the jockey and the groom) possess integrity: Will they remain loyal to the trainer? For instance, the apprentice jockey, under contract to a trainer, is perceived as being virtually incapable of a disloyal act—so faithful, it is said, that he will not divulge a secret under torture. An employer-trainer can conduct his secret activities in front of his "boy," treating his presence as a nonperson and having no fear of his selling out. And the seeker will not bother to approach the boy as a possible information source.

CONTROL MOVES

Recording moves are the preliminary aspects of the information game. In control moves, the information game advances to a higher level of sophistication. These more complicated moves are designed to throw the seeker off the scent. Once the trainer is aware of the seeker, this more involved orientation to the game begins.

Briefly, control moves refer to the "process of managing information about the situation." [4] For instance, as soon as the trainer knows his betting activities are under scrutiny, he may

4. *Ibid.*

employ a beard. There are two major kinds of impression management—covering and revealment. Covering, in turn, can be broken down to several strategic devices, as I now will illustrate.

One covering device is "open privacy," whereby seekers are kept away from an area where they can glean strategic information—but no effort is made to conceal that secretive activities are occurring. The most obvious of such areas at the track is the backstretch, or shed row area. Strangers who pry about this area are challenged as to their motives for being there. Even a recognized horseman must have an excuse for his presence when he wanders over from his own barn area to the neighboring shed. A more interesting example of open privacy is the paddock. Here a norm obliges competing trainers in a race to disattend from the activities and conversations between trainer and jockey that occur in the paddock stalls. Note, however, that while the trainer can expect to conceal his plans from the other trainers in the race, he is giving off expressions that other spectators (the pro, for example) can read as reliable information and as a warrant for his own course of action. Here, then, is an example of how successful covering with respect to one seeker in the information game is unsuccessful with respect to another seeker.

When the trainer resorts to some kind of camouflage so that seekers will misperceive his intentions, we may say that he is employing the covering device of "concealment." The trainer who rubs sand on a horse or bandages its legs before sending the animal to the paddock is attempting to give the impression that his horse is unfit, an inference others will make by observing the animal's "listless" coat or "crippled" legs. Here the trainer wishes to camouflage a good horse. At other times, he will want to make a bad horse look good (in hopes that someone will put in a claim), and so the horse will be polished and braided, dropped down in class, and ridden by the leading boy at the meet. In this manner, the trainer has managed the impression that his horse is fit—a horse worthy of being claimed. Just as the trainer has a rich repertoire for revealing false signs to offset the seeking activities of fellow horsemen, so too has he a repertoire to mislead the pros who are following his betting activities: making a

$2 bet while his beard is stuffing the $50 window is one such example of the trainer's effort at concealment.

To prevent an information leak, the trainer may resort to *postponement.* For instance, the trainer waits until entering the paddock before revealing his intentions to the jockey. Similarly, the trainer waits as long as possible before placing his bet. By waiting as long as possible to begin a course of action, he restricts the number of persons who can be tipped off as to his intentions.

While covering is undoubtedly the most common type of control move, occasionally the trainer will find it appropriate to employ its apparent opposite: "revealment." Here the trainer is purposefully disclosing information, but it is still part of his effort at impression management. When the trainer has a first-rate 2-year-old in his barn with already exposed form, he will do whatever he can to publicize how good his horse is, sometimes calling in the press to announce that his is the best 2-year-old since so-and-so. In the actual race, he will instruct the jockey to press the horse to win by the greatest possible margin. By this move, the trainer wishes to discourage other trainers from entering their animals in the often-overloaded 2-year-old stakes races. And since 2-year-old stakes are weight-for-age events (and hence the track handicapper can't penalize a strong performance with excess weight), the situation is structurally conducive for the employment of the revealment strategy.

The covering moves employed by the trainer are not unlimited, but structured by five fairly well-defined constraints.

One such restriction is that of *knowledge.* The trainer, for example, may not know what cues the seeker will use for making reliable inferences. It is in part because of this constraint that the pro is able to read typifications of the trainer's behavior in the paddock as a source of information as to his intentions.

A second constraint placed on covering is *self-control.* At times a person finds it hard to manage his "poker face." For example, when the jockey is getting instructions to run stiff, he typically looks inner-absorbed or directs his gaze around the paddock, unwittingly expressing that this race will be of little interest to him. The trainer, too, as the horses near the post, may find that his normal expressive vigilance is beyond management. Because the game is played before the scrutiny of others, interested parties therefore may glean clues as to the trainer's designs.

A sociologically more significant constraint on covering is *situational control*. For instance, the trainer can't avoid giving instructions to the jockey in the paddock, thus revealing the former's intentions. In addition, the trainer can't avoid working the horse in preparation for a race; he may decide on the pole from which the workout begins, but he cannot decide not to work the horse. In other words, there are situations—indeed, ecological areas—in which the trainer is forced to relax his normal role vigilance in order to proceed in a course of action. These situational controls weigh heavily in the favor of seekers who are intent on gleaning reliable information.

Another constraint on covering is the existence of *moral norms*. For instance, norms prevent a trainer from communicating statements that he himself does not believe. And so a trainer will never tell anyone that his horse has a good chance of winning when his intentions are solely to exercise the animal in a race. Conversely, if the horse has a good chance to win, he will not say that it is out for exercise. The trainer typically says nothing, leaving it to others to glean what they can about his intentions and his horse's capabilities.

A final constraint involves questions of *strategy*. One of the obvious risks faced by the trainer engaged in covering is that his efforts to manage impressions will be discovered *as such*. Once the seeker knows the trainer is employing strategy, he is in a better position to glean his intentions. For instance, if a horse is spotted in the morning with a shiny coat and "tight" ankles, but brought to the paddock in the afternoon with a dull coat and bandages, the seeker knows at once that an effort at covering has taken place, and he can infer what the trainer has in mind. Thus the trainer may find it unwise to take the risks that arise from covering.

UNCOVERING MOVES

In uncovering moves, the seeker appreciates that the trainer will try to influence his decision by the management of impressions (that is, control moves). The seeker, then, must take into account that the trainer takes into account that the assessments of the seeker takes into account that the trainer is engaged in the management of strategic information. At this point, the information game has become a bit sticky.

One type of uncovering move is to subject the trainer to an examination. A characteristic of an examination is that the trainer knows his activities are subject to scrutiny. Because the essence of training a horse (that is, getting the animal ready for a race) is the morning workouts, his training procedure will be one such activity open to examination. Other trainers and the betting public will be gleaning clues as to the trainer's intentions as a result of their focused observations or reports by clockers. One type of examination, then, is simple observation.

A more intimate form of examination is the interview. Once the horses have stepped on the track to parade toward the post, the trainer emerges from the paddock to take his place somewhere in the grandstand, clubhouse, or turf club to observe the race. During this time, the trainer may be approached and—consistent with the race track norm of mutual accessibility—asked a question. If bluntly asked, "How's your horse going to do?" the trainer will reply, "He has a chance," "It's a tough race," or "You can never tell." No information is communicated by these equivocal remarks. On the other hand, indirect questioning sometimes pays off. If, for instance, the trainer is asked why he has stationed himself so high up in the stands, making it necessary (by implication) for him to walk so far to the winner's circle, he may respond with useful information, saying: "No chance of that" or "It's going to be worth it."

Sometimes the interview is designed to break down the trainer and *force some kind of confession*. This is a prerogative and frequent activity of the officials. A former trainer relates this account:

> When you are called before the judges, they don't bawl you out, or anything like that. They act like perfect gentlemen and show you every courtesy. In a kindly manner, they will ask you to just tell them something about a certain case. Well, that's bad enough, and you try to get your bearing, but before you have time to think they will ask you to tell them something first about what took place at a certain time in a previous case. With things going from bad to worse, you have a very uncomfortable feeling.
>
> Then, as a gentle reminder, they will say that in case we should fail to mention it later, we would like to have you tell us something about another case, of what you said in the presence of two sociable gentlemen who won your confidence at a certain time and place after telling you they had been on the inside and cashed big bets on the race you won. This final blow comes like a bolt out of a clear sky and you are stunned that you stand there like a tongue-tied idiot wishing you could drop through the floor.[5]

A second type of uncovering move is spying. In the case of spying, unlike examinations, the trainer is observed when he feels that he is not subject to scrutiny. In the TRPB, horse racing has a professional spy force, and the trainer who comes under its surveillance gets the full James Bond treatment. As already mentioned, the TRPB is almost wholly staffed by former FBI and counterintelligence men, masters at bugging devices, tailing, and disguises. The trainer's only real defense against these professional agents is his knowledge of their existence. Thus he is suspicious of everybody. When a man comes around the barn and asks for a job walking hots or mucking stalls, the trainer considers the possibility that this scruffy-looking fellow may be a former air force colonel who cracked the German code.

Still another type of uncovering move is "seduction"—a move made, for instance, by the businessman jockey who gets the trainer to believe he is working with him to ready the horse for

5. Louis Pauer, *Suggestions with Facts and Figures on Horse Racing* (Cleveland: Hinchcliffe, 1938), p. 20.

a win. Seduction is also the uncovering device used by hotel men who operate establishments that cater to horsemen. These hotels offer special rates for trainers. The hotel man presents himself as someone who loves horse racing and who appreciates an occasional tip on the horses to make a small, recreational bet. In actuality, the betting activities of some of these hotel men constitute their major source of income. Trainers are also subjected to seduction in the commonly understood sense of the term. For several years, one of my own sources of inside information was an employee of a liquor store who got his information from the store owner who employed an attractive girl for the purpose of seducing trainers who purchased their *Forms* in the evening at this store. I was informed that the store owner got the idea from other liquor-establishment operators located near race tracks who hired attractive girls for the purpose of seducing unwary trainers and thus, Mata Hari fashion, obtain information.

A final uncovering move is coercive exchange, or pressures to force the trainer to cooperate, either by blackmail, bribery, or physical threats. While the following example of coercive exchange appears to me to no longer be a typical part of the contemporary racing scene, I include it for illustrative purposes:

> It does not require a great stretch of the imagination to make a fairly close guess of what might pass between a horseman and the representative of big betting or handbook interests. Mr. A, the trainer of a horse entered in a certain race, calls up Mr. X to inform him that he believes he can win. "I don't think you can beat B" is the response. "But," Mr. A objects, "I have beaten that horse before, and it's about time for me to win a race with my horse." "B's horse is now in the best condition" is the reply, "and you had better scratch, but if you start I wouldn't bet a nickel on your chances." That settles it as far as Mr. A's trying is concerned. In his judgment it might be better policy to accept orders, rather than offend Mr. X and his connections." [6]

The employment of these uncovering moves—examination, spying, seduction and coercive exchange—are somewhat restricted

6. *Ibid.,* p. 23.

by a set of constraints similar to those imposed on the trainer in his covering moves.

One constraint on the seeker's efforts at uncovering is his state of knowledge. For instance, the track veterinarian is continually on the lookout for sore-legged horses (whose condition is indicated by their manner of walking) to be placed on the "vet's list" and thus barred from racing at a particular meet. But he has no way of detecting the horse that has been de-nerved (an illegal procedure), permitting the horse to walk in a manner that does not give the appearance of being (as horsemen put it) "ouchy." Some trainers are also alert to pharmacological advances in search of stimulants that do not show up in the routine saliva tests.

Another constraint arises from the norms of the game. For instance, the rules of the game constrain the manner in which examinations are conducted. Thus the saliva test is typically given only to the horse finishing first. A trainer can take advantage of this routine examining procedure by stimulating his animal and giving the jockey firm instructions to finish second.

A final limitation arises from questions of strategy; for the employment of uncovering techniques may arouse the suspicion of the trainer leading him to greater concealment, as when he uses a beard to undercut the pattern of uncovering moves employed by bookies and others.

RECOVERING MOVES

In this final move in the information game the trainer "assumes that his cover will be suspected and so will try to provide in a doctored form just that evidence that [the seeker] is likely to use as a means of checking up on covers." [7] Note the re-covering move in this example: A trainer knows that a clocker knows that he will try to outfox him by working horses in a team, and breaking them at different poles in the hope that the clocker will miss or incorrectly time the workout. The trainer employs his usual strategy but—and here is the re-covering move—he

7. Goffman, "Strategic Interaction and Communication," *op. cit.*

stimulates (by drugs or by use of a battery) his animal so that it works impressively. The clocker will report back to his interested party that the trainer tried to hide the fast workout of a sharp animal, but that he, the clocker, caught the workout. The trainer employed his re-covering move so that the word will go around concerning his "speedy" animal and that someone will claim or offer to buy what is in fact an unsound or very ordinary horse. Therefore, what is the best evidence for the seeker is also the best evidence with which the trainer can tamper.

Although my illustrations of the information game have been taken from the arena of horse racing, its application very likely may be equally fruitful in other social arenas. But let me emphasize once again that the above description of types of moves in the information game is highly tentative. It may serve, however, as a suggestive guideline for the theoretical specification of other kinds of games—face games, relationship games and exploitation games.

Finally, I hope more sociologists will come to see that, for a clearer understanding of social interaction, the game's the thing.

Appendix:

HORSE RACING AND THE PROBLEM OF RATIONALITY

To analyze the problem of rationality, one must first clarify the various meanings of "rationality" and then show the empirical and theoretical consequences for alternative formulations.[1]

THE MEANINGS OF "RATIONALITY"

Sociologists have not attempted to compile an exhaustive list of various meanings of rationality, but any such list will include the following:

First, "rationality" is used to describe behavior that is "reasonable." So far as individuals in their everyday lives conduct themselves in a "reasonable" way, we say their behavior is

1. This discussion draws heavily on the writings of Alfred Schutz and Harold Garfinkel. See especially Schutz, "The Problem of Rationality in the Social World," in A. Brodersen (Ed.), *Collected Papers* (The Hague: Martinus Nijhoff, 1964), pp. 64–90; and Garfinkel, "The Rational Properties of Scientific and Common Sense Activities" in N. F. Washburne (Ed.), *Decisions, Values and Groups,* Vol. 2 (New York: Pergamon Press, 1962), pp. 304–312.

"rational." [2] Here the opposite of rational behavior is irrational behavior, strangeness, or insanity. Some situations are governed by a norm of rationality, and in those situations to be rational and to behave reasonably are not synonyms but identities.

Second, "rationality" is used to describe behavior that is taken to be "deliberate." Here deliberation involves the type of behavior described by Dewey as "a dramatic rehearsal in imagination of various competing possible lines of conduct."

Third, "rationality" is used to describe "planned" or "projected" behavior—the type found in the student who maps out the stages of his career from undergraduate training, to medical school to residency; or the man who weekly banks a portion of his pay to save for a down payment on a house.

Fourth, "rationality" is used to describe "prediction-making" behavior. When individuals are engaged in predicting the direction or outcome of events, their activity is described as "rational."

Fifth, and for us, finally, "rationality" is used to describe a "logical" activity. Here "logical" is used in the traditional philosophical sense, or as in the deductive models of scientific theorizing.

Throughout this study, I have indicated that actors involved in horse racing are engaged in rational behavior. To say that they are behaving rationally refers to behavior in any of the first four meanings.

To begin with, I have emphasized that a norm of rationality governs the betting activities of players. This norm is fulfilled so far as players "dope out" their own selections, rely on a system, or have presumable access to shrewd inside sources. The open use of magical practices is ridiculed and even when used they are disguised to appear as a rational procedure. When a player says, for instance, that he has a hunch that a certain horse will win

2. This first meaning of rationality can be thought of in terms similar to the concept of "freedom" discussed by the philosopher J. L. Austin. That is, to say we acted "rationally" is to say only that we acted *not* unrationally. "Rationality" is used only to rule out the suggestion of some or all of its recognized antitheses. Rationality is not a name for a characteristic of actions, but the name of a dimension in which actions are assessed. See J. L. Austin, "A Plea for Excuses," in *Philosophical Papers* (London: Oxford University Press, 1961), p. 128.

a race, he immediately supports his hunch by indicating in the *Form* that the horse in question is "dropping in class" or has the highest speed rating among the various entrants, etc.

The dramatic rehearsals that form another mode of rationality are standard practice for the pro. Recall Pittsburgh Phil's account:

> I think about them [the horses] the very first thing when I awaken, weighing them in one light and from one standpoint and another. As I dress and eat my breakfast, I am placing them here and there, giving each a chance until at last from all standpoints I decide which one, in a truly and perfectly run race, devoid of the hundred or more unlooked for incidents that can happen, should be the winner.

Rationality as projected action is the very core of one type of player whose motto is "you can't beat the race, but you can beat the races." His systematic method of selecting and playing is a mode of rationality similar to that of the insurance actuarial. His planned action is designed for long-range activity. Trainers, too, must engage in projected action in bringing, in some cases, a yet-unborn colt up to a race where it has been nominated.

Rationality as prediction-making behavior is the essence of the form-addict. His knowledge of the history of horses and his analysis of those sets of factors that brought about a situation in the past are used as a basis for the prediction of an event.

With the possible exception of the fifth meaning of "rationality" (that is, as "logical" behavior), to which we will now turn, the other types of rationality are aspects of the "attitude of everyday life" and examples are clearly abundant in the behavior of the social actors at the race track.

ALTERNATIVE FORMULATIONS

The alternative formulation to the "rationalities of everyday life" is the application of the logical model.

> In a word, the [logical] model furnishes a way of stating the ways in which a person would act were he conceived to be acting as an ideal scientist. The question then follows:

What accounts for the fact that actual persons do not match up, in fact rarely match up, even as scientists? In sum, the model of this rational man as a standard is used to furnish the basis of ironic comparison; and from this one gets the familiar distinctions between rational, nonrational, irrational, and arational conduct.[3]

What, then, would be the consequences of using this conception of rationality with specific reference to horse racing? In essence what I wish to do here is to compare the ethnographic mode of describing rational behavior with the logical mode.[4]

Presumably if the actor behaved rationally, according to the logical model, he would be using the most efficient means, as determined by scientists, to bring about a desired end. Let us take, for instance, the question of "beating" the races. According to the logical model, the scientific investigator, if he had knowledge of the relevant variables, could construct a set of "real" odds aimed at reflecting the actual chances of the various animals in the race. Employing a logical model, then, the investigator should be able to furnish a description of rational behavior superior in its accuracy to that which the actors would be capable of providing.

In my view, however, a logical model would either be divorced from the realities of the social world, or assume the existence of an ideal-typical actor, who is in fact the subject of the ethnographic model. To substantiate this claim, let us investigate how the scientific observer would construct the probabilities (the true odds) of the outcome of the race. This is a crucial consideration, since it is the estimate of probabilities (true odds) of a horse's winning that constitutes the professional gambler's advantage and ability to beat the game.

The logical model, in attempting to locate the true odds, can be broken down to two subtypes: the *urn*, or pure probability model; and the *statistical* model. To begin with, the race may be

3. Garfinkel, "The Rational Properties of Scientific and Common Sense Activities," *op. cit.,* p. 320.
4. The following discussion draws heavily on an unpublished paper written with Charles Fisher. For a more detailed analysis of the issues raised here see "On Rationality and the $2 Bet."

conceptualized as an urn filled with colored balls. The outcome of the race is determined by selecting a ball at random out of the urn. The number of different colors of the balls is equal to the number of horses in the race; each horse has a specific color. The distribution of the colors in the urn represents the *a priori* odds of any particular horse winning (that is, the odds that inhere in nature in some sense).

The players, of course, are betting in accord with their feelings on the probable chances of the various horses winning. Simplifying things somewhat, we can measure the worth of any of the bettor's personal system of odds by contrasting them to the actual (or *a priori*) odds. This is done in two stages. First, the bettor looks at the odds at post time and compares them with his personal odds. On the basis of this comparison, he constructs a strategy that maximizes his expectations of winning and then places his bets according to that strategy. On repeated trials, he will make money if his odds (estimate of probability of winning) in some sense closely approximate the *a priori* odds of the race (given, say, a somewhat random behavior of the other bettors). How good the gambler's odds are is determined by comparing them mathematically to the *a priori* odds of the outcome of the race.[5]

Now the urn model makes some questionable assumptions about the situation. The most important of these assumptions is that the race represents a uniformly repeatable event, possessing an actual set of probabilities. Since horses, jockeys, and trainers in each race are dissimilar, a horse race has little to make it comparable to an urn model. Further, the actual odds of the outcome of the race are not given as they are in the case of an urn, so that there is no ideal with which we can compare the odds developed by the public.

The second subtype of the logical model, the statistical model, is designed to compensate for the difficulties of the urn model.

5. In order to say how good the odds of the bettor are, we must first decide upon a notion of good—a metric on the space of distributions—and then find a distribution that will be considered the actual or real probabilities. The "goodness" of a bettor's personal probabilities is measured by the distance of his distribution from the ideal one.

This model is based on the purely probabilistic one, but attempts to take into account the fact that the horse race is not a uniform event. The statistical model tries to smooth over the irregularities of everyday life and to reduce them to a point where it is reasonable to consider events as if they were ruled probabilistically.[6]

To establish whether the class of bettors who considers themselves experts—the pros—have what are to be considered the true set of odds on the outcome of the race, we need to construct an *a priori* set of odds against which to measure the pro's odds. There are several ways of doing this. We can experiment by running the race over and over again. Of course, this is out of the question in the real world. Or we can look over the results of previous races and draw out of them similar conditions and events that will stand in place of our repeated experiment. That is, we can look to the histories of the different horses and, by emphasizing certain aspects and leaving out others, construct an idealized repetitive race involving the horses that are competing in the current race, so as to establish what the probable outcome will be.[7]

To make this historical study of the horses, a sophisticated statistician will not confine himself to the data published in the *Racing Form*, and even if he does he will seek out an expert to teach him how to read the *Form*. In other words, to establish statistically what the *a priori* odds of the race are, the statistician will seek out an expert to help him accumulate factors relevant to establishing uniformly repetitive events from which a set of *a priori* odds may be derived. Once the statistician has these odds, he proceeds exactly as in the urn model; he uses the same mathe-

6. We are here considering what could be called a Bayesian statistical model.

7. In fact, this is the way some betting system builders proceed. One very sensible and mathematically sophisticated system builder, Paul Fabricand, in his book *Horse Sense* (New York: David McKay, 1965) talks about each bet as if it were a policy adopted for a series of exactly similar races. The percentage of victories in this idealized run becomes a property of the horse when the bettor constructs an overall strategy. Interestingly, the pros do not regard races as random events. They are not gamblers as craps shooters or blackjack players are. In fact, they do not take part in these activities. The pro regards a race, aside from accidents, as a predictable event. If he errs, there is an accountable reason.

matical techniques to determine how good the bettors' different odds are.

One feature of this model is that, to evaluate the "accuracy" of the probabilities of any bettor, the statistician must construct a set of actual odds (that is, reduce the situation to the urn model); and to construct these *a priori* odds, the statistician must address himself to the histories of the horses, preferably with the aid of an expert. What this implies will be made clear after examining the ethnographic model.

The ethnographic model postulates two distinct domains: first, the race itself, the outcome of which determines how the funds wagered are to be distributed; second, the arena in which the players make up their minds and bet on the race. The first domain is mostly irrelevant to our discussion. Granted it constitutes a very rich descriptive world; but as it effects how the pool of wagers is distributed, it can be seen to be just some event that takes place and that indicates who the winner is. Otherwise put, we can say that after the final bets have been placed, it makes little difference how the event is decided; for it is in the arena of the players that the ratios of distribution have been established.

Turning to this arena, we again find various groups of participants acting on the basis of their information about the horses and the odds posted on the parimutuel board. Their decision to bet rests on the odds they construct from their feelings of the likely outcome of the race and the posted odds. The bettors, then, address themselves to the histories of the different horses and to the activities of their fellow bettors.

Those persons whom we distinguished as pros conceive of themselves as more able than others to collect information about the likely performances of the respective horses and to dope out a profitable strategy for betting. In placing bets, the pro relies on such sources as the *Racing Form*, his evaluation of the intentions of the trainers, any information he can buy, his knowledge of how the world of the race track operates, and so forth. This is a "living" world in which the *Form* is merely a helpful tool not a definitive document of the horses' histories. Furthermore, the horse itself is perceived as being as live and variable as any of the other actors on the scene. The animal's history is a "human" history, accompanied by the feelings and desires of the various people (the owner, the trainer, the jockey) who interact with it.

In an ethnographic description of the race track, these same considerations of the pro are taken into account. Each factor helps to constitute the world of the race track as constructed by its inhabitants. Moreover, whatever odds appear within this world do so in the minds of the actors: the odds on the parimutuel board are a result of how the bettors place their bets; the odds on which the players act are constructed by them out of the materials they come across. There are no real odds of the event because, for the actors, the event just takes place. It is a unique happening, something with particular space-time coordinates. After the event has taken place, the actors address themselves to it as "the horse race that has been run" and construct evaluations of the race on the basis of their stakes in it and what they saw during the running. The events of the race itself can be taken as more material for ethnographic description and be treated as such. What I am stressing here is that the race took place along with all of its fortuitous characteristics. Neither the actors nor the observer possess a single natural model of the race. The race is a nonrecurrent event, not just in the trivial sense that each race is unique, but in the sense that no race like this—in terms of horses, riders, track conditions, etc.—has been or will ever be run. As such, there is no immediate way to construct abstract probabilities of the outcome. The only probabilities present are those diverse odds created by the human actors who are taking part in the unfolding of events.[8]

If we compare the three models we find distinct styles of description: the urn model reduces the world to that which is

8. A much harder case to argue is that of coin-tossing, in which there is a natural, commonly accepted rational model. For real gambling situations, such as casinos, we have almost no ethnographic material against which to view the probabilists' model. From what we surmise about gambling establishments, we would guess that the points being made here are also applicable.

uniformly repeatable; the statistical model (the second subtype of the logical model) sees the world as irregular and attempts to reduce it to regularity by selection and smoothing; the ethnographic model takes the world as it is constructed by the various actors (including the observer) and looks to the structures they impose upon the world while carrying out their intended activities.

The first two modes of (logical) description carry with them certain presumptions. The urn model baldly assumes a "logically" rational world. Since the case we are considering lacks a uniformity of event, this model does not fit the domain we wish to describe. The statistical model looks to selected regularities in the world to secure a rational description. But to find regularity in the world, one must turn to the actors of that world for guidance. As we saw earlier, the statistician—in attempting to establish the *a priori* odds as to the outcome of the race— looked to the official histories of the horses and employed an expert to read the histories properly and supply other kinds of information. In other words, to establish regularity so as to construct a rational model of the situation, the statistician is forced to take the position of one of the players. That is, if the statistician wishes to construct a logical model to measure the reality of the probabilities of the bettors, he must resort to the activities of the bettor or employ one of their number to tell him what is important, as well as the likely odds of the race.

Here we have the crux of the matter. In attempting to rationalize the world of the race track, the mathematical, statistical, or "scientific" man must take his place with the bettors at the track. Despite his ability to gather and sort information, the statistician cannot establish any more real set of probabilities than those established by the actors themselves. He is bound to the world of actors, and must proceed in exactly the same way as the other subjects; he cannot lift himself out of the world of events as constituted by the participants; he has no way of obtaining a superior reality from his constructions. In examining how logical modes of description are applied to the race track, one readily sees that the logical model does not become an abstract measure of the actions of the participants. Just the opposite is true: The logical model as descriptive of the events is under-standable only in terms of what the participants themselves do.

Let us note that these remarks are not to be taken as a refutation of the use of the logical model. (These models provide guides to action and are no more refutable than, say, the strate-gies of a revolutionary.) Nevertheless, my position here is that rational descriptions reside in the human communities in which they are made and therefore must be seen in terms of the struc-tures of those communities.

On the basis of these remarks, we conclude with Harold Garfinkel:

> No necessity dictates that a definition of rational action be decided in order to conceive a field of observable events of conduct. This result has the important and paradoxical con-sequence of permitting us to study the properties of rational action more closely than ever before. Instead of using the vision of the ideal scientist as a means for constructing descriptive categories of behavior—and rational, nonrational, irrational and arational are such categories—the rational characteristics of activities may be addressed with the empir-ical task of describing them as they are found separately [as types] of rationalities or in clusters of these characteristics.[9]

The reader, I hope, will consider the implications of this dis-cussion for the contemporary debates concerning the use of mathematics in the study of social behavior, and the question of whether the study of social life should proceed from the actor's or observer's point of view.

9. Garfinkel, *op. cit.*, p. 321.

INDEX

a

Addict (handicapper), 87–94, 96–97
Adequate description, criterion of, 5–6, 8
Ainslie, Tom, 26, 33
Arcaro, Eddie, 44
Atkinson, Ted, 23, 26, 34
Austin, J. L., 172

b

Backstage, 22–24, 71, 75
See also Offstage; Onstage
Backstretch personnel, 71–73
See also Jockey, career of
"Bad actor," 23
See also Horses, qualities of
Bargaining. *See* Social exchange
Barnard, Chester I., 48
Bartlett, F. C., 95
Bateson, Gregory, 1
"Beard," 50–52, 75–76
See also Strategies of trainer
Beating the game, system, or race, 4, 84–85
lay theories on, 119–25

See also Rationality
Becker, Howard S., 28, 94
Beliefs, persistence of, 18–19, 27, 91–92, 131
Bellringer, 101–102, 155
Bergler, Edmund, 87
Betting, 105
handling money, 121–25
primary wager, 58
secondary play, 58
See also Bookie; Daily double; Information; Tipping; Owners; Rationality; Trainer
Betting percentages, 98–100
Blanche, Ernest E., 105, 148
Bloch, Herbert A., 116
Bookie (bookmaker), Ch. 7, 50–51, 57–59, 94, 98–100, 107–108, 131–32
horse room (bookie joint), 139, 143–44
louse (or flea) book, 139–42
organized book, 139, 142–43
Breeding, 21–22
Bridge jumper, 98, 153
See also Gamblers
Broderson, A., 6, 171
Buck, Fred S., 109
"Bug" or "bug boy." *See* Jockey

Garfinkel, Harold, 22, 91, 171, 173–74, 180
"Getting even," 41, 124
See also "Covering one's bet"
Gluckman, Max, 134
Goffman, Erving, 3, 4, 5, 7, 22, 25, 72, 74, 88, 94, 103, 106, 113, 141, 159, 169
Goodenough, Ward H., 6
Gurwitsch, Aron, 114
"Gyp." *See* Honest Johns

h

"Halterman," 55, 64
Hart, H. L. A., 70
Headliner. *See* Honest Johns
"Heart," 18–22
See also Horse, qualities of
Herman, Robert D., xiii, 122, 123, 131
Hollander, E. P., 57
Homans, George C., 86
Honest Johns, 49, 54–55, 59–68
 "gyp," 49, 65–68
 headliner, 49, 59–64
 horsetrader, 49, 64–65
Honor, 20–21
See also Horse, qualities of
Horse, Ch. 2
 conditioning (or training) of, 48–49, 55
 identification of, 14, 104–105, 148, 154
 naming, 14, 150
 other terms for, 13, 18, 21, 23, 38, 65
 qualities of, 18–21, 22
Horsetrader. *See* Honest Johns

i

Impression management, 39, 43–44, 54, 163–70
See also Communication strate-gies; Information; Information game
Information, Ch. 1
 ambiguity in, 2
 and betting activity, 58–59, 126
 certainty and uncertainty of, 81–87, 104–105, 130, 134, 139, 144
 definition of, 1
 espionage, 51–52, 104–105
 inside (or hot), 57, 95, 102, 111, 118, 129, 132
 interactional ignorance, 1
 organization of, 3
 organizational ignorance, 1, 130
 self-destroying, 4, 58, 83, 119, 136
 tipping, 52–53, 68, 97, 102
 touting, 129–30
See also Information game; Ma-nipulator; Syndicate man; Trainer, instructions to jockey
Information control. *See* Communi-cation strategies; Impression management; Paddock; Strate-gies
Information game, 4, 50–52, 132, 158–70
 control moves, 162–65
 recording moves, 160–62
 recovering moves, 169–70
 uncovering moves, 166–69
See also Manipulators, lone wolf; Pittsburgh Phil
Insider, 102–103, 129–30

j

Jockey, Ch. 3
 age, 28–30, 37–38
 betting activities of, 38
 "bug," 30
 career of, 28–34
 character, 25–27
 communication strategies, 43–44
 expenses, 32–33
 fees, 32, 36
 Negroes, 27